Table of Contents

Background and Overview

This 2013 Measuring Broadband America—February Report contains the most recent results from the Federal Communication Commission's (FCC) Measuring Broadband America program. This program, whose first results were published in August 2011, is an ongoing, rigorous, nationwide study of residential broadband performance in the United States. This study, like those conducted before, involves actual performance tests for thousands of subscribers of Internet Service Providers (ISPs) serving well over 80 percent of the residential market. Our initial Measuring Broadband America Report presented the first broad-scale study of actual consumer broadband performance throughout the United States. This effort was followed approximately a year later by a second report, released in July 2012, and now the present report.

As explained in the accompanying Technical Appendix, each report in this series is based on measurements taken during a single reference month that has been chosen to represent a typical usage period for the average consumer. The reference month for the first report was March 2011, and the collection period for the second report, initially set for March 2011, was shifted to April 2012 to ensure collection of a sufficient amount of valid data. The reference month for this report is September 2012, five months after the previous testing period. As such, we present this as a supplemental report, noting that substantive network change is best measured in years, not months. Going forward, we plan to repeat testing each year in the month of September, and transition to annual reporting.

In this report, we are pleased to include results on satellite technology for the first time, based on test results collected from ViaSat, a major satellite services provider.[1] While in the past we have collected and released raw data on satellite performance, we have not reported on test results from this technology, as we recognized that the industry was on the verge of a major transition. In 2011, the satellite industry began launching a new generation of satellites offering performance as much as 100 times[2] superior to the previous generation, leading to the entry of new satellite-based broadband providers. Consequently, we are now able to include comparisons between satellite and wireline technologies in this report.

Overview of reported results

This Report provides an update on data collected in April 2012 and released in our July 2012 Report.[3] That Report found that five ISPs routinely delivered nearly one hundred percent or greater of the speed advertised to the consumer,[4] even during time periods when bandwidth demand was at its peak, while the average ISP delivered 96 percent of advertised download speed during peak usage periods.[5] This February Report is based on data collected in September 2012, which represents a five month interval from the previous data collection. In the September 2012 testing period, ISPs on average delivered 97 percent of advertised download speeds during peak periods, statistically equivalent to the last report. Overall, we found results in this report materially unchanged from the previous report with one exception, Frontier Communications, which has improved its performance 13 percent from the last reporting period. Encouragingly, we find that another trend previously observed in the July 2012 Report has also continued, as consumers have sustained their migration to higher speed services. In this report for the first time we tested download speeds as high as 75 Mbps (megabits per second), and we know that even higher rates are being offered by service providers to their customers.[6]

Based on the results of this report, we make three primary observations regarding the current state of residential broadband service in the United States.

1. Many ISPs continue to closely meet or exceed the speeds they advertise.

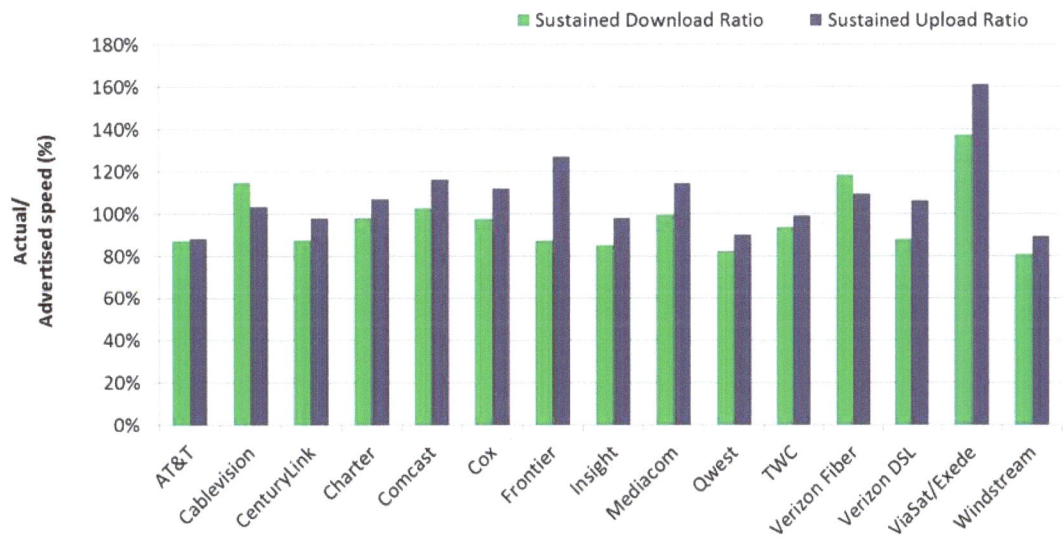

The chart above provides a comparison of upload and download performance during peak usage periods across all ISPs. During the short period of time that has elapsed since the last measurement period, we find that, with the exception of Frontier's significant improvement in advertised versus actual performance, performance levels of ISPs have remained largely unchanged. As observed in the July 2012 Report, the majority of ISPs continue to closely meet or exceed the speeds they advertise, although some ISPs fell short of delivering speeds that matched their advertised rates.

2. Consumers are continuing to migrate to faster speed tiers.

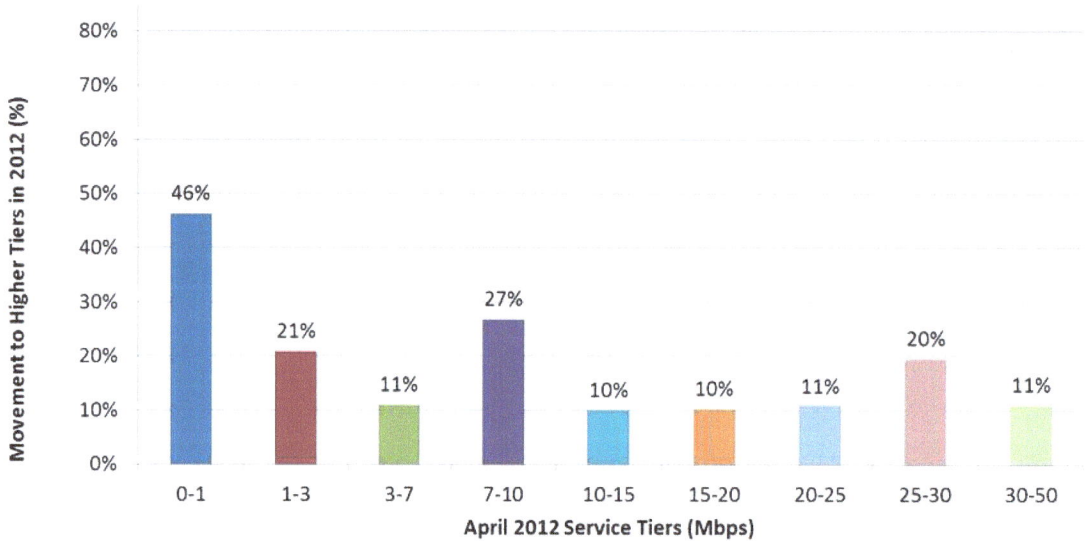

This chart shows that consumers are moving to faster speed tiers, continuing the trend that we highlighted in the July 2012 Report. The bars represent the percentage of volunteers from each of the April 2012 tiers that moved to a higher speed tier by the September 2012 testing period. ISPs also continue to upgrade their networks to provide faster and faster speed tiers. We are encouraged that we are now testing service tiers up to 75 Mbps and plan to evolve our testing program to include even higher tiers as they are rolled out by providers and adopted by consumers. In our tests of download speed, we added five new tiers above 30 Mbps from the last testing period,[7] and our tests of upload performance included one additional offering above 8 Mbps.[8] In this report, we find the average subscribed speed is now 15.6 Mbps, representing an average annualized speed increase of about 20 percent.

3. Satellite broadband has made significant improvements in service quality.

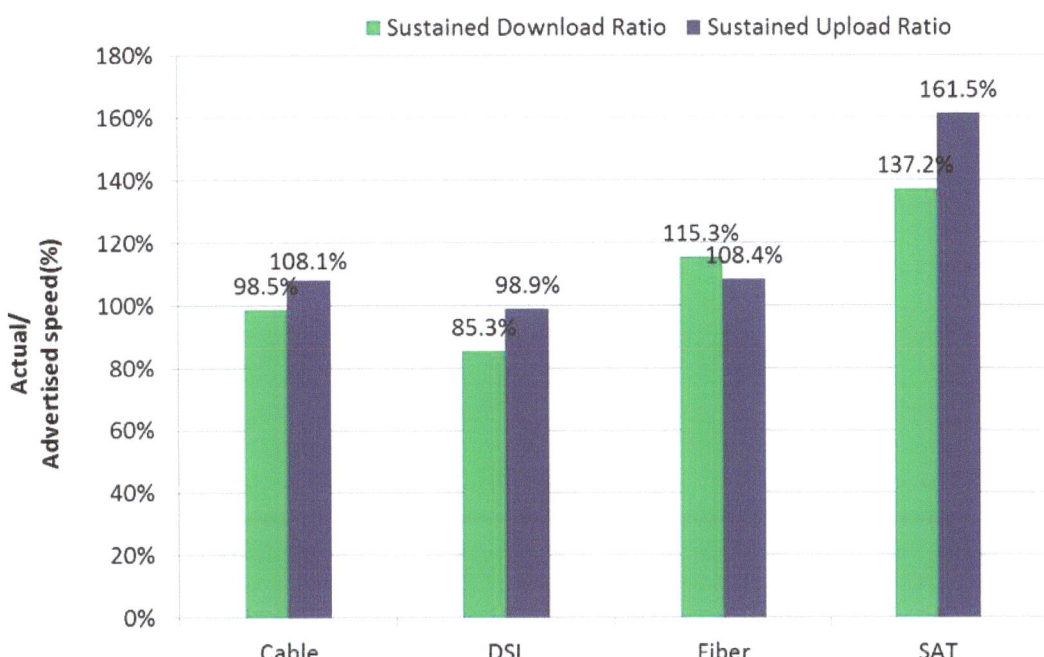

As the chart above depicts, there is some variation by technology in actual versus advertised speed during peak usage periods, with satellite returning the highest performance ratio. In the past, satellite broadband faced certain technological challenges not experienced by wireline technologies. Previous generations of satellites had limited bandwidth, which restricted the speeds available to the consumer. In addition, due to the physical characteristics of satellite technology, latencies are significantly larger than for terrestrial technologies. Starting in 2011, the consumer broadband satellite industry began launching a new generation of satellites which have greatly improved overall performance. As relevant here, the high capacity of ViaSat's ViaSat-1 satellite, which at the time of launch surpassed the total capacity of all current Ku-, Ka-, and C-band satellites over North America,[9] together with other technological improvements discussed below, have decreased latency and improved the quality of satellite broadband service available to subscribers. In our testing, we found that during peak periods 90 percent of ViaSat consumers received 140 percent or better of the advertised speed of 12 Mbps. In addition, both peak and non-peak performance was significantly higher than advertised rates. While latency for satellites necessarily remains much higher than for terrestrial services, with the improvements afforded by the new technology we find that it will support many types of popular broadband services and applications.

Background on the production of the Report

As with the previous Measuring Broadband America reports, this Report relied on measurement hardware and software deployed in the homes of thousands of volunteer consumers by our contractor, SamKnows. Although the SamKnows "Whitebox" devices and their software conduct automated, direct measurements of broadband performance throughout the year,[10] all testing represented in this Report was conducted in September 2012. The Report focuses on four ISP delivery technologies—DSL, cable, fiber,[11] and satellite. The study examines service offerings from 14 of the largest broadband providers,[12] which collectively account for well over 80 percent of all U.S. residential broadband connections. This Report focuses on the major findings of this study, while a separate Technical Appendix recounts the process by which these measurements were made and describes each test that was performed. The structure of this Report and the measurements represented herein largely track the July 2012 Report, which we hope will provide a useful baseline for comparison.

We continue to emphasize in many of the charts and metrics our defined peak usage period of weeknights between 7:00 pm to 11:00 pm local time, as opposed to a 24-hour reporting period. We believe that focusing on the peak usage period provides the most useful information for consumers because it demonstrates the kind of performance users can expect when the largest number of people are accessing the Internet and delivery of Internet service is under the most strain. While we measure other time periods and include the results of these off-peak tests in data sets that will be released to the public, we use peak usage period performance for the purpose of comparing ISPs.

Throughout this Report we use the term "advertised speed" to refer to the speed ISPs use to advertise and market a particular broadband service. We also use the term "sustained speed." On a short time scale, broadband speeds or information rates may vary widely, at times approaching or even exceeding advertised speeds and at other times—due to network congestion—slowing to rates that may be well below advertised speeds. To provide an estimate of long-term average broadband performance, in this Report we indicate "sustained speed," which is speed averaged over a period of several seconds.[13]

It is important to note some limitations on the results contained in this Report. Generally only the most popular service tiers among an ISP's offerings were tested, even though some service providers may offer other tiers not represented by volunteers contributing data to the program.[14] In addition, the data are only analyzed at the national level, and are not collected in a way that permits meaningful conclusions about broadband performance at the local level.[15]

The basic objective of the Measuring Broadband America study is to measure broadband service performance as delivered by an ISP to the consumer. Although many factors contribute to end-to-end consumer broadband performance, this Report focuses on those elements of the Internet pathway under the direct or indirect control of a consumer's ISP on that ISP's own network: from the consumer gateway—the modem used by the consumer to access the Internet—to a nearby major Internet gateway point. Thus, any bandwidth limitations or delays incurred in the consumer's home or in segments of the Internet outside an ISP's network are not reflected in the results. This focus aligns with key attributes of broadband service that are advertised to consumers and allows a direct comparison across broadband providers of actual performance delivered to the household. It also constitutes that network portion for which the consumer is paying a service fee to their ISP.

The activity of producing this report has given rise to benefits beyond its mere publication. We have taken advantage of the consensus among the participants of this program to jointly, along with members of industry, propose broadband performance measurement standards we believe will be of future benefit to consumers.[16] In addition, service level performance metrics based upon the work of the Measuring Broadband America program are being incorporated into other programs of the Commission. We are encouraged that many broadband providers have found this ongoing measurement study sufficiently valuable to adopt our methodology, develop their own internal broadband performance testing programs, and make improvements to their ongoing disclosures to consumers.

Major Findings of the Study

- **Actual versus advertised speeds.** The July 2012 Report showed that the ISPs included in the Report were, on average, delivering 96 percent of advertised speeds during the peak consumer usage hours of weekdays from 7:00 pm to 11:00 pm local time. The February 2013 Report finds little change from this, with a calculated average for the report of 97 percent.[17] Only one service provider had a significant change: Frontier improved its performance by 13 percent.

- **Sustained download speeds as a percentage of advertised speeds.** The average[18] actual sustained download speed during the peak period was calculated as a percentage of the ISP's advertised speed. This calculation was done for each speed tier offered by each ISP.

  - *Results by technology*:

    - On average, during peak periods DSL-based services delivered download speeds that were 85 percent of advertised speeds, cable-based services delivered 99 percent of advertised speeds, fiber-to-the-home services delivered 115 percent of advertised speeds, and satellite delivered 137% of advertised speeds. This compares to July 2012 results showing largely the same performance levels: 84 percent for DSL, 99 percent for cable, and 117 percent for fiber. These results suggest that many ISPs are meeting established engineering goals for their respective technologies.

    - Peak period speeds decreased from 24-hour average speeds[19] by 2.4 percent for fiber-to-the-home services, 4.0 percent for DSL-based services, 4.2 percent for cable-based services and 4.4 percent for satellite services. This suggests a very slight decrease across all technologies, when compared to the results reported in July 2012 of 0.9 percent for fiber services, 3.5 percent for DSL services and 3.9 percent for cable services.

o **_Results by ISP:_**

▪ Average peak period download speeds per ISP varied from a high of 137 percent of advertised speed (Viasat/Exede) to a low of 81 percent of advertised speed (Windstream). These results are largely consistent with the July 2012 Report, although as previously noted satellite was not included in prior reports. The only ISP to show significant change was Frontier which showed a 13 percent relative improvement, going from 77 percent of advertised speed to 88 percent of advertised speed.

▪ In the July 2012 Report, we found that, on average, ISPs had a 3 percent decrease in delivered versus advertised download speed between their 24 hour average and their peak period average. In the September 2012 testing period, average performance decreased slightly, and there was a 3.9 percent decrease in performance between 24 hour and peak averages.[20] This would be consistent with higher demands on network usage across consumer participants and we emphasize that while it suggests a slight trend, September 2012 numbers are consistent with those included in the July 2012 report.

- **<u>Sustained upload speeds as a percentage of advertised speeds</u>.** With the exception of three providers, upload speeds during peak periods were 98 percent or better of advertised speeds. On average, across all ISPs, upload speed was 108 percent of advertised speed, closely matching results in the July 2012 report of 107 percent.[21] With the exception of satellite technology and consistent with previous reports, across all carriers upload speeds showed little evidence of congestion with little variance between 24 hour averages and peak period averages. Satellite showed a 6 percent drop in performance from 24 hour average to peak period, but still remained above 100 percent.

  o **_Results by technology:_** On average, satellite services delivered 161 percent, fiber-to-the-home and cable-based services delivered 108 percent, and DSL-based services delivered 99 percent of advertised upload speeds. These compare with figures from the July 2012 Report of 110 percent for cable, 106 percent for fiber, and 103 percent for DSL.

  o **_Results by ISP:_** Average upload speeds among ISPs ranged from a low of 88 percent of advertised speed to a high of 161 percent of advertised speed. In the July 2012 Report, this range was from a low of 91 percent to a high of 122 percent.

- **Latency.** Latency is the time it takes for a packet of data to travel from one designated point to another in a network, commonly expressed in terms of milliseconds (ms). Latency can be a major controlling factor in overall performance of some Internet services. In our tests, latency is defined as the round-trip time from the consumer's home to the closest[22] server used for speed measurement within the provider's network. In the February 2013 report, across all terrestrial technologies during peak periods, latency averaged 29.6 ms comparable to the July 2012 Report figure of 31 ms.[23] Satellite systems involve the transmission of information over long distances and have correspondingly higher latencies than for terrestrial technologies. ViaSat had a measured latency of 638 ms for this report, approximately 20 times that for the terrestrial average.

  o During peak periods, latency increased across all terrestrial technologies by 10 percent, which represents a modest drop in performance.[24] During the April 2012 testing period this figure was 6.5 percent. Since satellite latency is dominated by the transmission distances involved, it shows no practical (less than 1 percent) variance between peak and 24 hour periods.

    - *Results by technology:*

      - Latency was lowest in fiber-to-the-home services, and this finding was true across all fiber-to-the-home speed tiers.

      - During the September 2012 testing period, fiber-to-the-home services provided 18 ms round-trip latency on average, while cable-based services averaged 26 ms, and DSL-based services averaged 44 ms. This compares to figures from the April 2012 testing period of 18 ms for fiber, 26 ms for cable and 43 ms for DSL.

    - *Results by ISP:* The highest average round-trip latency for an individual terrestrial service tier was 67.7 ms (Windstream), while the lowest average latency within a single service tier was 13.8 ms (Cablevision). This compares to the previous report's maximum latency of 70.2 ms and minimum of 12.6 ms.

- **Effect of burst speed techniques.** Some cable-based services offer burst speed techniques, marketed under names such as "PowerBoost," which temporarily allocate more bandwidth to a consumer's service. The effect of burst speed techniques is temporary—it typically lasts less than 15 to 20 seconds—and may be reduced by other broadband activities occurring within the consumer household.[25] Burst speed is not equivalent to sustained speed. Sustained speed is a measure of long-term performance. Activities such as large file transfers, video streaming, and video chat require the transfer of large amounts of information over sustained periods of time. Sustained speed is a better measure of how well such activities may be supported. However, other activities such as web browsing or gaming often require the transfer of moderate amounts of information in a short interval of time. For example, a transfer of a web page typically begins with a consumer clicking on the page reference and ceases when the page is fully downloaded. Such services may benefit from burst speed techniques, which for a period of seconds will increase the transfer speed. The actual effect of burst speed depends on a number of factors explained more fully below.

- o Burst speed techniques increased short-term download performance by as much as 79 percent during peak periods for some speed tiers. The benefits of burst techniques are most evident at intermediate speeds of around 8 to 15 Mbps and appear to tail off at much higher speeds. This compares to July 2012 Report results with maximum performance increases of approximately 118 percent. However, this seeming drop in performance is largely the result of ISPs migrating their customers to higher speed tiers where burst techniques become less effective. Accounting for this, results are largely consistent with the July 2012 Report.

- **Web Browsing, Voice over Internet Protocol (VoIP), and Streaming Video.**

  - o *Web browsing.* In specific tests designed to mimic basic web browsing—accessing a series of web pages, but not streaming video or using video chat sites or applications—the total time needed to load a page decreased with higher speeds. However, this performance increase diminishes beyond about 10 Mbps, as latency and other factors begin to dominate and limit performance. For these high speed tiers, consumers are unlikely to experience much if any improvement in basic web browsing from increased speed–*i.e.*, moving from a 10 Mbps broadband offering to a 25 Mbps offering. This is comparable to results reported in July 2012 and suggests intrinsic factors (e.g., effects of latency, limitations inherent in protocol used for web browsing) limit overall performance at higher speeds. It should be noted that this is from the perspective of a single user employing a web browser, and that higher speeds may provide significant advantages in a multi-user household or where a consumer is using a specific application that may be able to benefit from a higher speed tier.

  - o *VoIP.* VoIP services, which can be used with a data rate as low as 100 kilobits per second (kbps) but also have latency and jitter requirements, were adequately supported by all of the service tiers discussed in this Report.[26] However, VoIP quality may suffer during times when household bandwidth is shared by other services. The VoIP measurements utilized for this Report were not designed to detect such effects.

- o ***Streaming Video.*** February 2013 Report test results suggest that video streaming will work across all technologies tested, though the quality of the video that can be streamed will depend upon the speed tier. For example, standard definition video is currently commonly transmitted at speeds from 1 Mbps to 2 Mbps. High quality video can demand faster speeds, with full HD (1080p) demanding 5 Mbps[27] or more for a single stream. Consumers should understand the requirements of the streaming video they want to use and ensure that their chosen broadband service tier will meet those requirements, including when multiple members of a household simultaneously want to watch streaming video on separate devices.[28]

- **Variability of Performance.** In the July 2012 Report, we added a new category of charts to track variability of performance of a service provider, which we continue in this Report. We have calculated the percentage of users across a range of advertised speeds that experience, on average, performance levels at that speed or better. This information, commonly called a cumulative distribution function, shows how speed is distributed across the population of consumers included in this survey. As in the July 2012 Report, for February 2013 the result of this metric demonstrates that consumers should be reasonably confident that the performance they receive from their ISP will be consistent with the results included in this Report.

- **Satellite Broadband Services.** In this report we include for the first time test results for ViaSat, a satellite-based broadband service. Satellite-based broadband Internet services differ from terrestrial-based technologies in several key ways. First, because satellites broadcast wirelessly directly to the consumer, no actual terrestrial infrastructure has to be deployed. As a result, satellite technologies have a more uniform cost structure, which is unique among the technologies under study in our report.

Satellite facilities have historically had impairments which have limited their competitiveness with other broadband services. One such impairment was limited bandwidth, which reduced the service speeds that could be offered to consumers. In addition, latency associated with satellite service has been an order of magnitude greater than wireline broadband technologies. A geosynchronous satellite orbiting the earth at a distance of greater than 36,000 km has a round trip latency of about 500 ms.[29] The necessary signaling between the set-top box and the satellite controller, to request assignment of a communication channel, can double this to over 1000 ms, which would precluded use of many latency-sensitive services. In contrast, the maximum average latency found in our surveys for terrestrial technologies is less than 70 ms.

Because of these differences in technology, including the effects that latency can have on some services,[30] and differences in service offerings, direct comparisons between satellite services and terrestrial-based broadband services are difficult to make.

Beginning in 2011, the consumer broadband satellite industry began launching a new generation of satellites to significantly improve overall performance. In October of that year ViaSat launched itsViaSat-1 satellite, which has an overall capacity of 140 Gb/s.[31] In addition to increasing bandwidth capacity, ViaSat and other satellite industry operators have lowered overall latency by making improvements to other elements of their architecture, such as by dispensing with the need to request communication channel assignments, adopting advances in consumer satellite terminal equipment, incorporating protocol acceleration technology, and developing new error correction technology to provide resiliency to rain fade. Despite these many improvements, latency for this new generation of satellite-delivered broadband remains high.

Differences in service offerings also compound the difficulty of direct comparisons with the terrestrial-based offerings. Terrestrial-based service providers typically price by service speed rate with some ISPs additionally applying data caps that limit the amount of data that may be downloaded within a month. In contrast, ViaSat offers a single service rate and provides service tiers in the form of data caps at rates of 10 gigabytes (GB), 15 GB, or 25 GB per month,[32] with unmetered downloads permitted between midnight and 5:00 a.m. local time.

Online Resources

In conjunction with this study, the Commission will make the following associated resources available to the public and research community: electronic copies of the charts included in the Report; data sets for each of the charts in the Report; documentation regarding the underlying methodology by which the data was collected and calculated; tabular results for each test performed for each ISP across all speed tiers; data sets for all recorded tests that constitute the basis for the Report; and a complete raw data set for all tests run during the testing period.[33] In addition, the Technical Appendix describes the methodology used in the Report. The Commission is releasing this material in the hope that independent study of this data set will provide additional insights into consumer broadband services.

- **February 2013 Report**: fcc.us/mba0213report
- **February 2013 Technical Appendix**: fcc.us/mba0213appendix
- **Charts in February 2013 Report**: fcc.us/mba0213charts

- **Validated Data Set**: (for charts in February 2013 Report):
  fcc.us/mba0213validdataset

- **Methodology Resources**: (how data collected and calculated):
  fcc.us/mba0213methodology

- **Tabular Test Results**: (data sets recorded during the September 2012 testing
  period): fcc.us/mba0213testresults

- **Raw Bulk Data Set**: (complete, non-validated results for all tests run during the
  September 2012 testing period): fcc.us/mba0213rawbulkdataset

- **July 2012 Report, Technical Appendix, and Data Sets**:
  fcc.us/mba0712report

- **August 2011 Report, Technical Appendix, and Data Sets**:
  fcc.us/mba0811report

Description of Tests Included in Report

The February 2013 Report is based on 13 separate measurements that can be used to
characterize various aspects of broadband performance to the consumer. The ISPs that
participated in the study agreed to base the Report on a month of data, and participants in the
study agreed to September 2012 as the test month. September 2012 data were verified and
are analyzed in this Report. Active data collection continued after September, and while this
subsequent data set has not been verified or analyzed, it is included in the Raw Bulk Data Set
that will be released to the public.[34]

As in previous reports, this Report emphasizes two metrics that are of particular relevance to
consumers: speed and latency. Broadband throughput or speed is the primary performance
characteristic advertised by ISPs. Broadband speed is the average rate at which information
"packets" are delivered successfully over the communication channel. A higher speed
indicates a higher information delivery rate. A 10 Mbps service should deliver ten times as
much information as a 1 Mbps service in a given period of time.[35]

The use of transient performance enhancements such as burst techniques, which are available
as a part of many cable-based services, present a technical challenge when measuring speed.
Services featuring burst techniques will deliver a far higher throughput for short periods,
usually at the beginning of a download after a brief warm-up period. The duration of the
speed burst may vary by ISP, service tier, and other factors. For example, a user who has
purchased a 6 Mbps service tier might receive 18 Mbps for the first 10 megabytes[36] (MB) of a
particular download. As supported by our test, this is of significant benefit to applications
such as web browsing, which use relatively short-lived connections and transfer short bursts
of data. But once the burst window lapses, throughput will return to the base rate, making

the burst rate an inaccurate measure of performance for longer, sustained data transfers. In addition, other household broadband activities may decrease or eliminate the benefit of the speed burst. The speed test employed in this study isolated the effects of transient performance-enhancing services such as burst techniques from the long-term sustained speed, and the Report presents sustained and "burst" speed results separately. Consumers should evaluate the relevance of each capability based upon their specific needs—consumers who use broadband mostly to web browse might find the "burst" speed very relevant; consumers who download many large files might find it less relevant.

Latency is another key factor in broadband performance. For practical reasons, latency measurements typically represent the round-trip latency, *i.e.*, from the consumer to the measurement point and back.[37] The impact of latency is felt in a number of ways. For example, high round-trip latencies may compromise the quality of voice services in ways that are perceptible to consumers.[38] Even lower latencies, which may not be directly noticeable by human perception, can still degrade network performance. Computer networks and applications are more sensitive to latency than are humans. Latency affects the rate of information transmission for TCP protocol, which is commonly used to support Internet applications, and can therefore limit the maximum speed achievable for a broadband service regardless of the actual service speed. In the interactive communications found in computing applications, latency is also additive, which means that the delay caused by the sum of a series of latencies adds to the time it takes to complete a computing process. Thus, latency can have a significant effect on the performance of applications running across a computer network. As service speeds increase, the impact of network latency can become more noticeable, and have a more significant impact on overall performance.

One of the key factors that affects all aspects of broadband performance is the time of day. At peak hours, more people are attempting to use broadband connections to access the Internet simultaneously, giving rise to a greater potential for congestion and degraded user performance.

This Report highlights the results of the following tests of broadband speed and latency, as measured on a national basis across DSL, cable, fiber-to-the-home, and satellite technologies:

- **Sustained download speed**: throughput in Mbps utilizing three concurrent TCP connections measured at the 25-30 second interval of a sustained data transfer

- **Sustained upload speed**: throughput in Mbps utilizing three concurrent TCP connections measured at the 25-30 second interval of a sustained data transfer

- **Burst download speed**: throughput in Mbps utilizing three concurrent TCP connections measured at the 0-5 second interval of a sustained data transfer

- **Burst upload speed**: throughput in Mbps utilizing three concurrent TCP connections measured at the 0-5 second interval of a sustained data transfer

- **UDP latency**: average round trip time for a series of randomly transmitted user datagram protocol (UDP) packets distributed over a long timeframe

Overall, a total of 3 billion measurements were taken across 170 million unique tests.

Data derived from all tests performed is available on our website at http://www.fcc.gov/measuring-broadband-america.

Test Results

We present the summary of our findings below.[39] The Commission is separately releasing a Validated Data Set[40] on which this Report was based, and will also release a Raw Bulk Data Set of non-validated data collected outside the reference month. The results below are reported by performance variation, by ISP, and by technology (DSL, cable, fiber-to-the-home, and satellite) for the most popular service tiers offered by each ISP. As noted above, we focus on periods of peak consumption. The results presented below represent average[41] measured performance across a range of consumers, and while these results are useful for comparison purposes, they should not be taken as an indicator of performance for any specific consumer.

All charts below use data from September 2012 unless otherwise noted. We also include a chart comparing data from September 2012 and April 2012 (the data used in the July 2012 Report).

VARIATION BY ISP AND SERVICE TIER IN DELIVERY OF ADVERTISED SPEED

Chart 1 shows actual speed as a percentage of advertised speed both over a 24-hour period and during peak periods across all ISPs. In the September 2012 testing period, the majority of ISPs delivered actual download speeds during peak periods within 85 percent of advertised speeds or better, with modest performance declines during peak periods.[42] These results are largely indistinguishable from the July 2012 Report, with the exception of Frontier, which demonstrated an improvement of nearly 13 percent in the peak period.[43]

Chart 1: Average Peak Period and 24-Hour Sustained Download Speeds as a Percentage of Advertised, by Provider—September 2012 Test Data

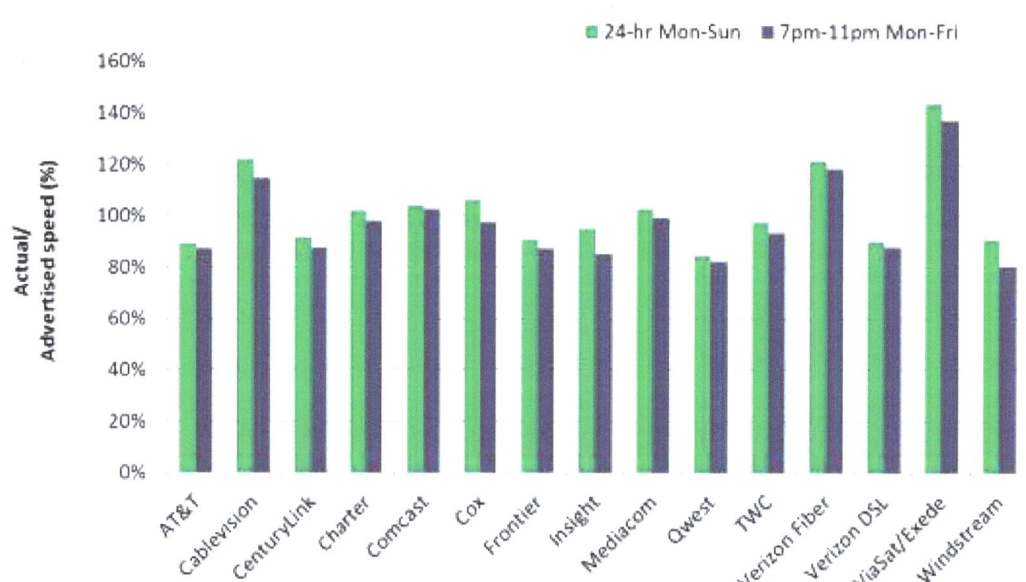

As shown in Chart 2, and as was also found in the previous report, upload performance in the September 2012 test data is much less affected than download performance during peak periods. Overall performance declined very slightly from the previous testing period. While in the April 2012 testing period almost all ISPs delivered above 100 percent or above of their advertised upload rate, in the September 2012 testing period six ISPs fell slightly short of 100 percent.

Chart 2: Average Peak Period and 24-Hour Sustained Upload Speeds as a Percentage of Advertised, by Provider—September 2012 Test Data

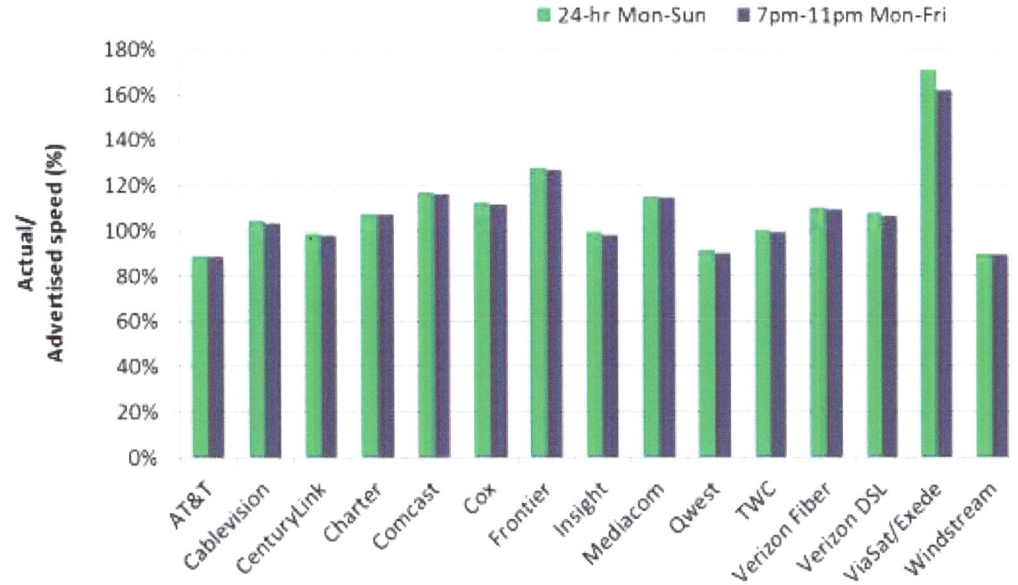

Chart 3 provides a comparison of upload and download performance during peak periods across all ISPs.

Chart 3: Average Peak Period Sustained Download and Upload Speeds as a Percentage of Advertised, by Provider—September 2012 Test Data

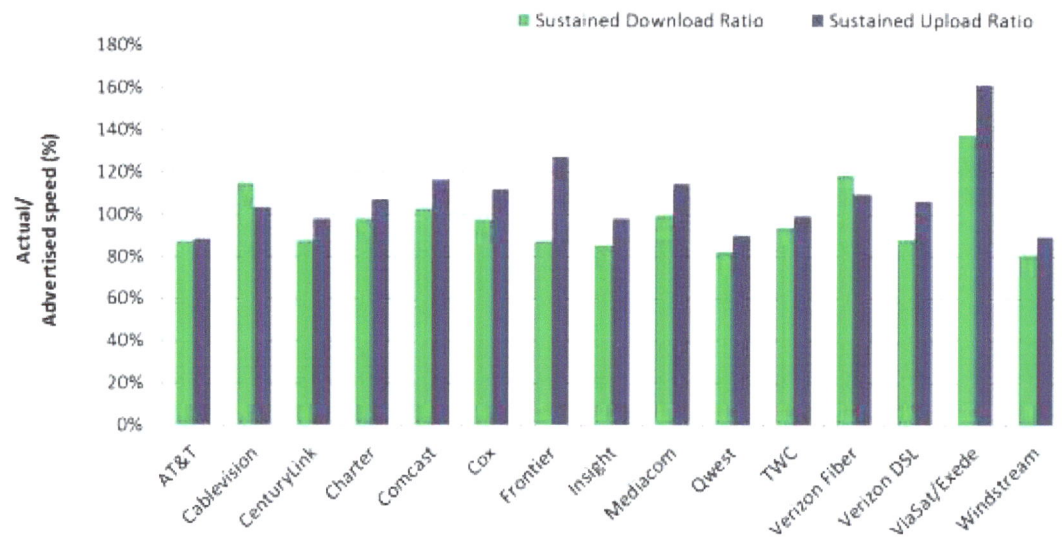

VARIATION BY ACCESS TECHNOLOGY IN DELIVERY OF ADVERTISED SPEED

The delivery of advertised speeds also varied by technology. As shown in Chart 4, which depicts results from the September 2012 test data, there is some variation by technology in actual versus advertised performance during peak periods. DSL on average meets 85 percent of advertised download speed during peak periods, compared to 84 percent in the April 2012 testing period; cable meets 99 percent, the same as in the July 2012 Report. Fiber-to-the-home performance decreased slightly, from 117 percent of advertised speeds in the July 2012 report to 115 percent of advertised speeds in the September 2012 testing period. Although satellite was not included in previous reports, during the September 2012 testing period the technology delivered 137 percent of advertised download speed. During peak usage, ISPs are generally better at delivering advertised upload performance than download performance.[44] Small changes were noted for upload performance, with cable going from 110 percent to 108 percent, DSL from 103 percent to 99 percent and fiber from 106 percent to 108 percent of advertised speed. Satellite delivered 161 percent of advertised upload speed.

Chart 4: Average Peak Period Sustained Download and Upload Speeds as a Percentage of Advertised, by Technology—September 2012 Test Data

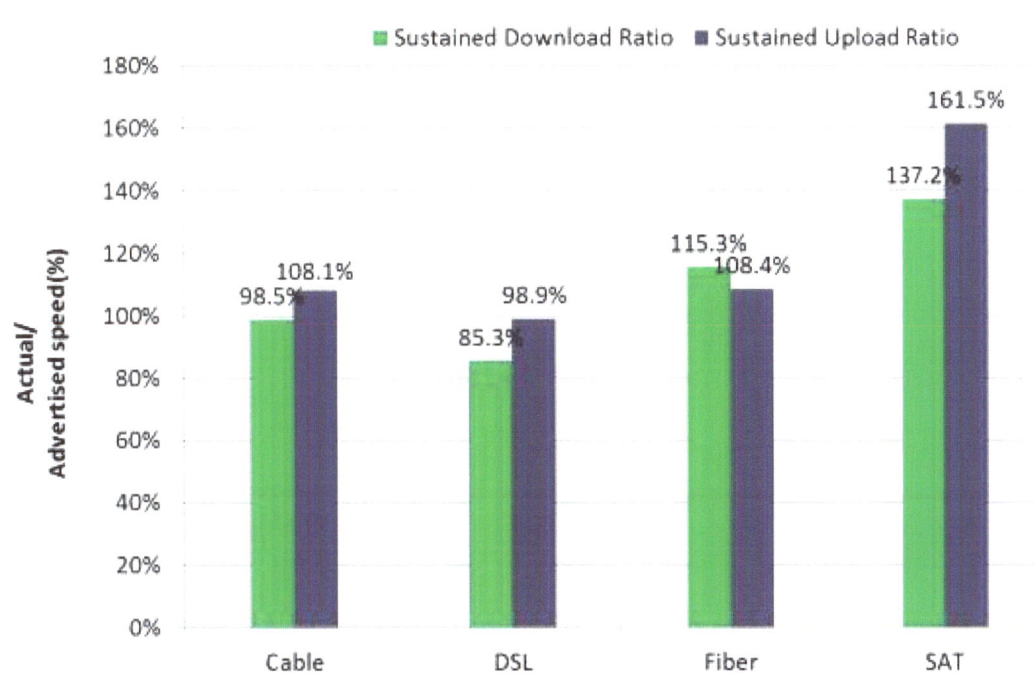

VARIATION BY SERVICE TIER IN DELIVERY OF ADVERTISED SPEED

Download Peak Period Throughput

As shown in Charts 5.1-5.5, peak usage period performance varies by service tier among ISPs included in this study during the September 2012 test period. On average, during peak periods, all ISPs deliver 80 percent or better with a majority of ISPs delivering performance 90 percent or better of advertised speeds.[45] However, performance varies among service tiers. For example, Windstream's 12 Mbps tier delivers 72 percent of advertised speed, a low across all ISPs and speed tiers. In contrast, Windstream's best performing service tier of 3 Mbps tier delivers 85 percent of advertised speed. Other ISPs provide service that is either close to or exceeds advertised rates. In the 5-10 Mbps tier, four ISPs returned results that were significantly better than those from the April 2012 testing period, with three providers showing similar improvements in the 12-15 Mbps speed tier.

Two different ISPs (Cablevision and Verizon), using different technologies (cable and fiber), were both able to deliver peak period speeds of 115 percent of advertised rates during peak periods, suggesting that engineering and deployment rules, in addition to technology, are a crucial component of overall service quality.

Chart 5.1: Average Peak Period Sustained Download Speeds as a Percentage of Advertised, by Provider (1-3 Mbps Tier)—September 2012 Test Data

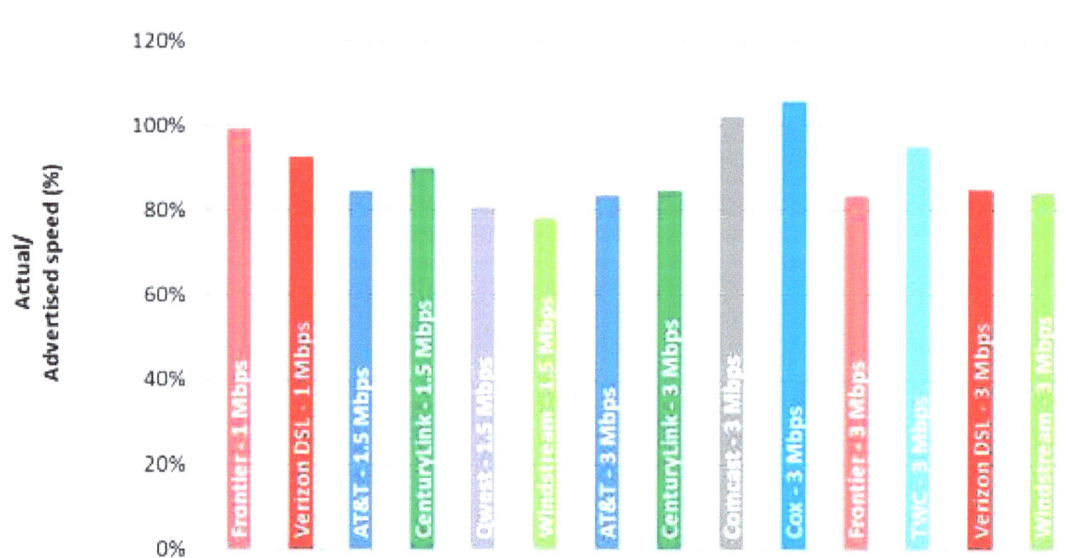

Chart 5.2: Average Peak Period Sustained Download Speeds as a Percentage of Advertised, by Provider (5-10 Mbps Tier)—September 2012 Test Data

Chart 5.3: Average Peak Period Sustained Download Speeds as a Percentage of Advertised, by Provider (12-15 Mbps Tier)—September 2012 Test Data

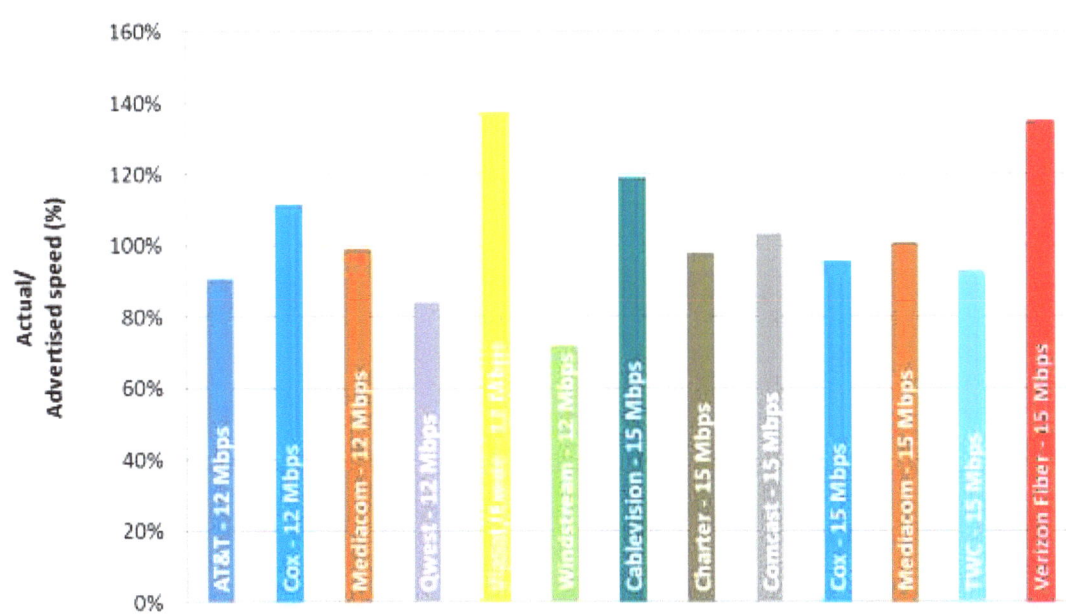

Chart 5.4: Average Peak Period Sustained Download Speeds as a Percentage of Advertised, by Provider (18-25 Mbps Tier)—September 2012 Test Data

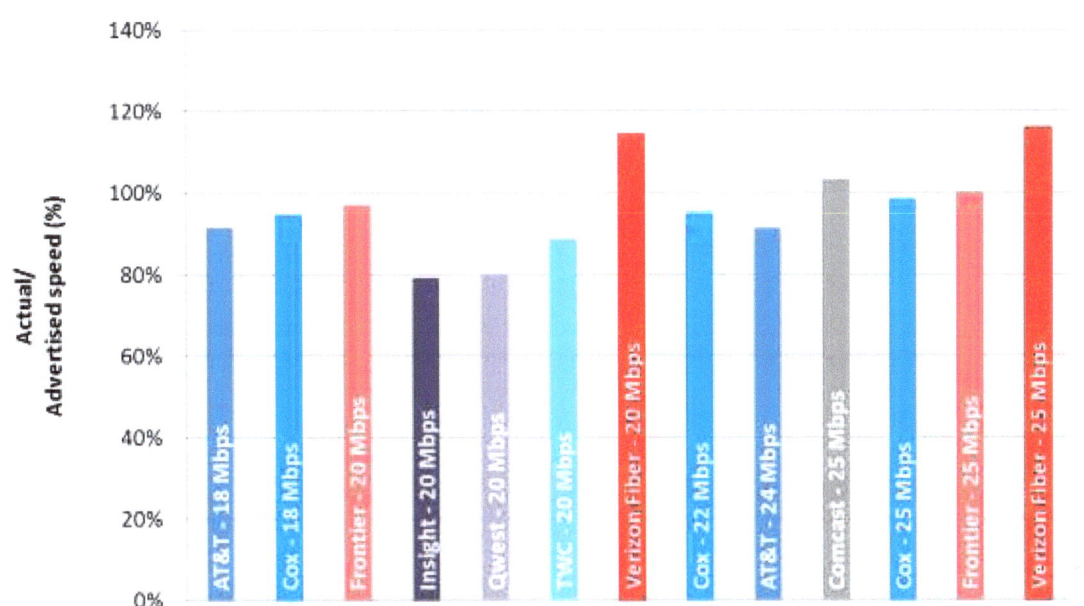

Chart 5.5: Average Peak Period Sustained Download Speeds as a Percentage of Advertised, by Provider (30-75 Mbps Tier)—September 2012 Test Data

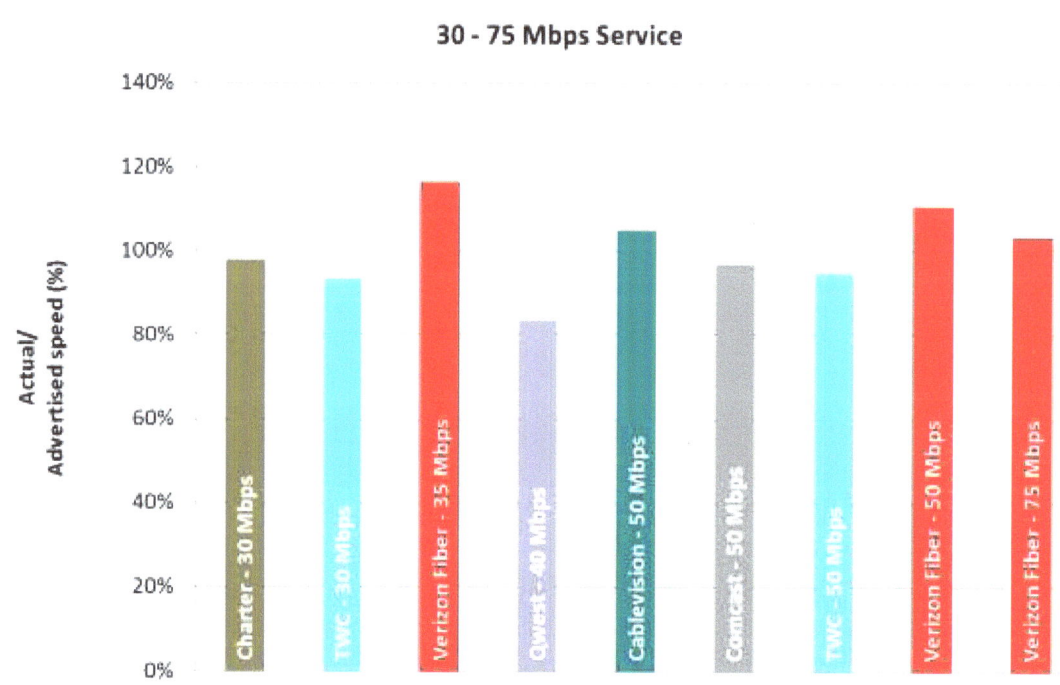

Upload Peak Period Throughput

Consumer broadband services are typically offered with asymmetric download and upload rates, with the download rate many times faster than the upload rate. The ratio of actual to advertised speed for upload performance is generally superior to the ratio measured for download performance. On average across all speed tiers, ISPs deliver 106 percent of the advertised upload rate, which is consistent with the 107 percent reported from the April 2012 testing period. In this Report we found that cable services delivered, on average, 108 percent of advertised upload speed versus 110 percent in the July 2012 report; fiber delivered 108 percent of upload speed, up slightly from 106 percent in the prior report; and DSL delivered 99 percent upload speed, down from 103 percent in the previous study. During the September 2012 testing period satellite technology delivered 161 percent of advertised upload speed. We found little evidence of congestion among upload speeds, with an average drop in performance between 24-hour week day and peak week day results of only 0.7 percent amongst terrestrial-based ISPs. Charts 6.1-6.4 depict average upload speeds for each ISP by service tier.[46]

Chart 6.1: Average Peak Period Sustained Upload Speeds as a Percentage of Advertised, by Provider (0.256-0.64 Mbps Tier)—September 2012 Test Data

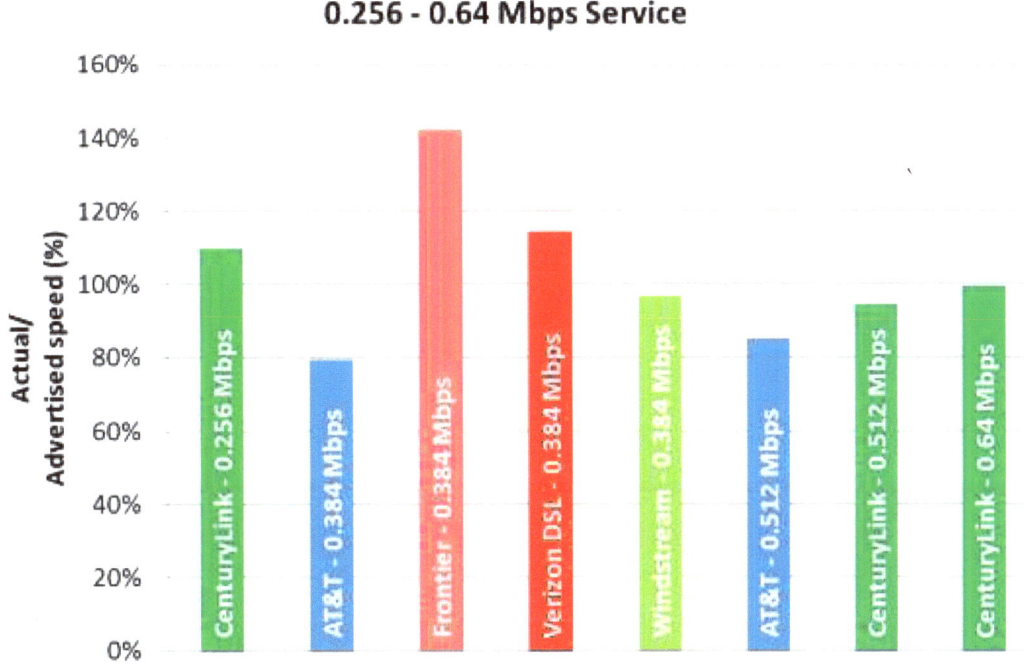

Chart 6.2: Average Peak Period Sustained Upload Speeds as a Percentage of Advertised, by Provider (0.768-1.5 Mbps Tier)—September 2012 Test Data

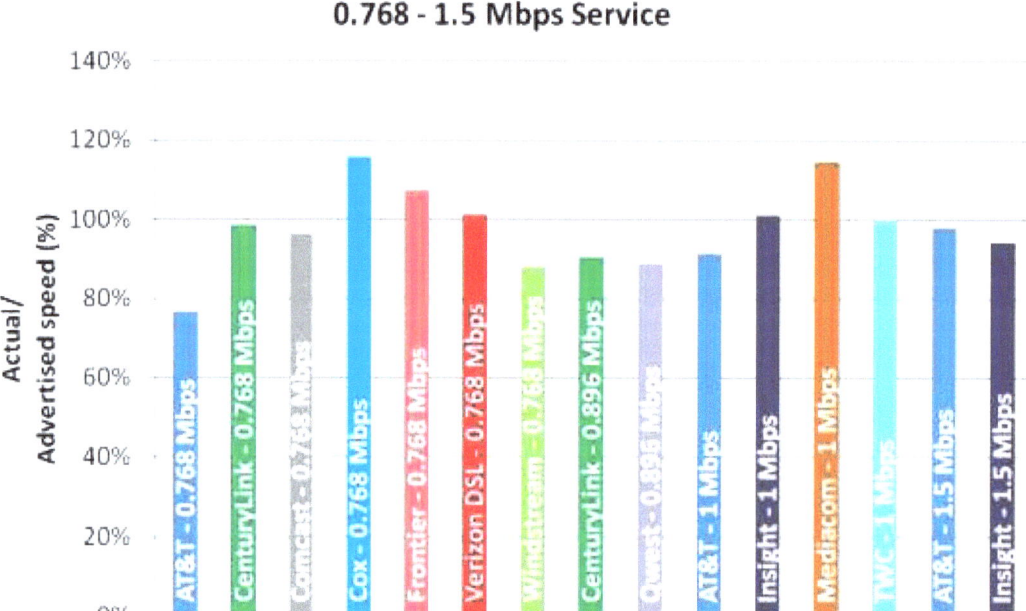

Chart 6.3: Average Peak Period Sustained Upload Speeds as a Percentage of Advertised, by Provider (2-5 Mbps Tier)—September 2012 Test Data

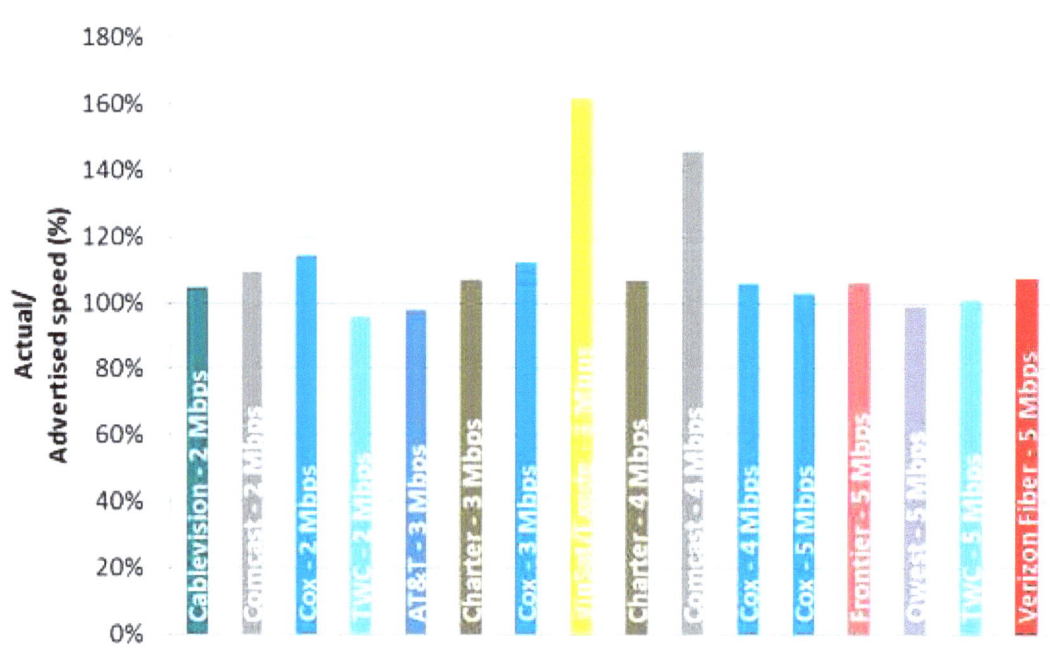

Chart 6.4: Average Peak Period Sustained Upload Speeds as a Percentage of Advertised, by Provider (8-35 Mbps Tier)—September 2012 Test Data

Burst Versus Sustained Download Throughput

Comparing burst download speeds versus advertised speeds demonstrates the effect that burst services have on data throughput. Technologies which do not generally employ burst technologies, such as DSL-, fiber-to-the-home, and satellite, showed no significant differences between sustained and burst measurements. Chart 7 below shows the percent increase that burst technology had during the September 2012 testing period on initial download performance, in those cases where the provider employs this technology.[47] To create this chart, for each ISP service tier included in our testing, we subtracted the sustained performance from the measured burst performance to highlight the difference between the two. This allowed us to spotlight performance increases created by burst technology. Results that showed a less than 10 percent improvement were discarded to make the chart easier to read. Thus, in Chart 7, cable services employing boost technology can be seen to temporarily increase performance by as much as 79 percent depending upon speed tier. The effectiveness of burst technology declines at the higher speed tiers, and overall burst technology showed less impact during the September 2012 testing period than in the previous report.

Chart 7: Average Peak Period Burst Download Speeds as a Percentage Increase over Sustained Download Speeds, by Provider Where Tiers Showed a Greater than 10% Increase—September 2012 Test Data

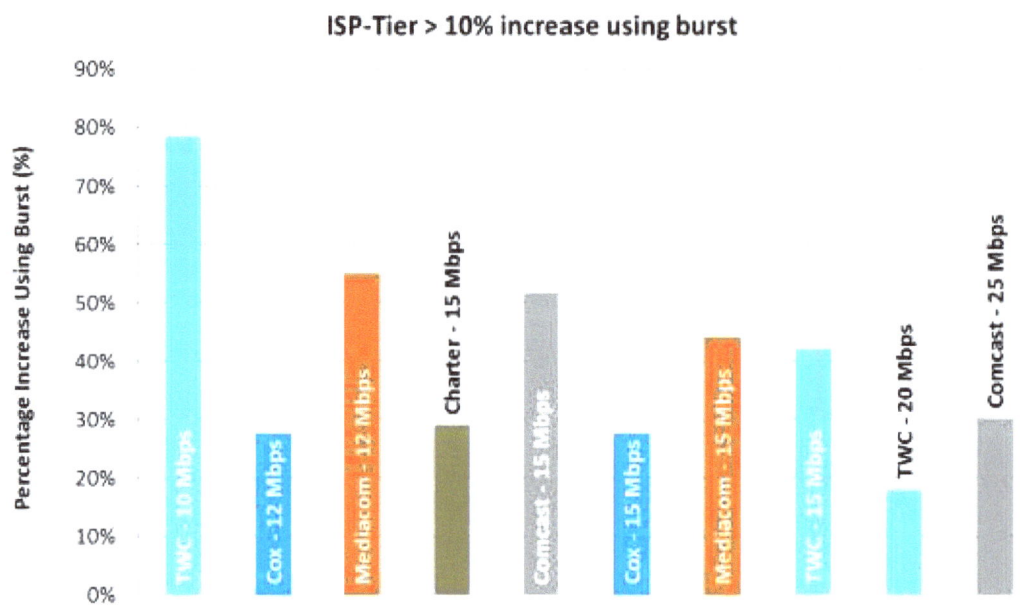

The use of transient performance boosting features is less prevalent for upstream connections. However, as shown in Chart 8, burst technology does appear to be applied to upstream performance by some ISPs. For example, in the 2 Mbps speed tier, Comcast shows an approximately 70 percent increase in performance in the burst test as compared to the sustained upload test.

Chart 8: Average Peak Period Burst Upload Speeds as a Percentage Increase over Sustained Download Speeds, by Provider (All Tiers)—September 2012 Test Data

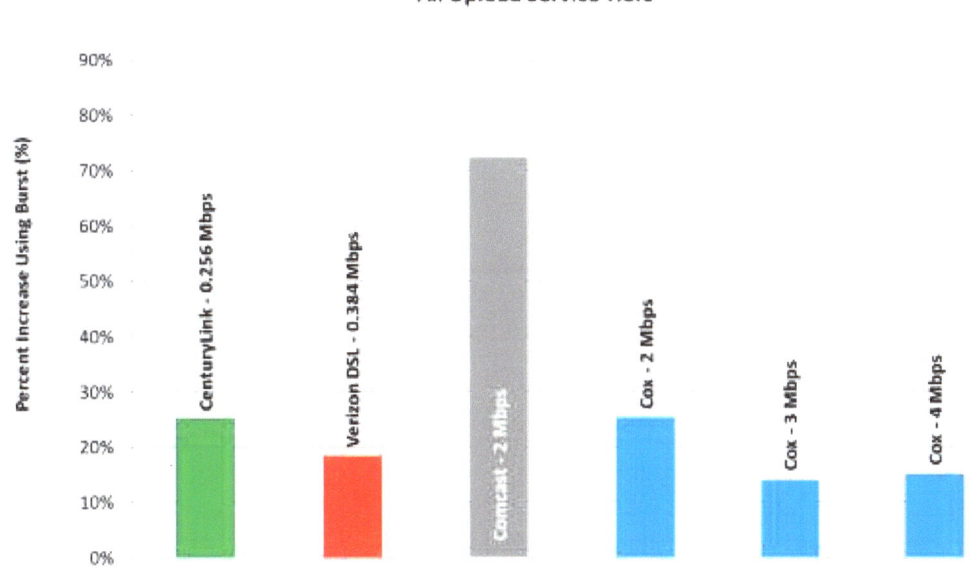

Chart 9 provides an overview of the average burst download and upload speed per ISP as a percent of advertised performance. We note that most ISPs do not employ a burst feature, and Chart 9 is presenting the results of the burst test across all ISPs. Therefore the performance of many ISPs will not be markedly changed from their sustained speed performance. Comcast continues to demonstrate the highest burst upload speed, reaching on average across all speed tiers 168 percent of advertised upload speed, while for download speed Comcast, Mediacom and TWC show noticeable increases of over 140 percent of advertised speed.

Chart 9: Average Peak Period Burst Download and Upload Speeds as a Percentage of Sustained Speed, by Provider—September 2012 Test Data

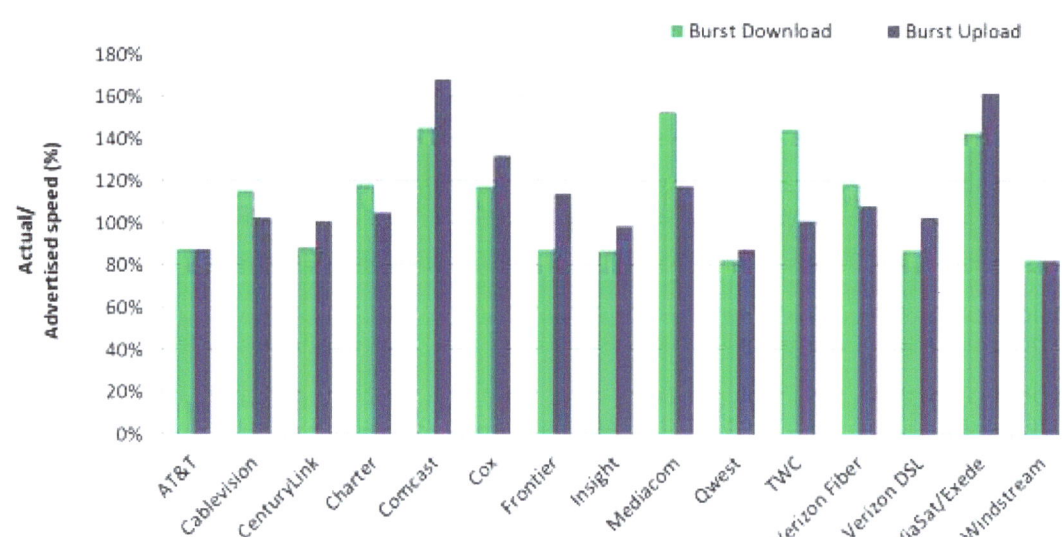

Latency

Latency test results in the September 2012 testing period remained, on average, little changed from the July 2012 Report although there were changes in individual speed tiers. We believe this is because in properly engineered networks the primary causes of latency are intrinsic to the service architecture and are primarily determined by load independent effects. As can be seen from Chart 10, and as was true in the July 2012 report, latency varies by technology and by service tier.[48] However, this relationship is complex. For example, average latency within a technology class is largely invariant within a range of speed tiers, although in general higher speed tiers have lower latency than lower tiers. The largest influences affecting latency are technology driven: from highest to lowest, satellite, DSL, cable, and fiber exhibit decreasing latency.

Also largely unchanged from previous findings, fiber-to-the-home, on average, has the best performance in terms of latency, with 18 ms average during the peak period, with cable having 26 ms latency and DSL 44 ms latency, virtually identical to the previous report. The highest average latency in a speed tier for a terrestrial technology was for DSL with 54 ms measured latency. The highest latency recorded for a single ISP using terrestrial technology was 68 ms, slightly down from 70 ms recorded for this same ISP in the April 2012 testing period. Satellite technology, due to the distances between the satellite and terrestrial points, recorded the highest overall latency of 638 ms.[49] While the test results found variance in latencies among technologies, the latencies measured here for all of the terrestrial-based technologies should be adequate for common latency-sensitive Internet applications, such as VoIP.[50] As noted, the situation is more complex for satellite, and dependent on a number of factors, including application sensitivity to latency and user perception of latency's effects.

Chart 10: Average Peak Period Latency in Milliseconds, by Technology—September 2012 Test Data

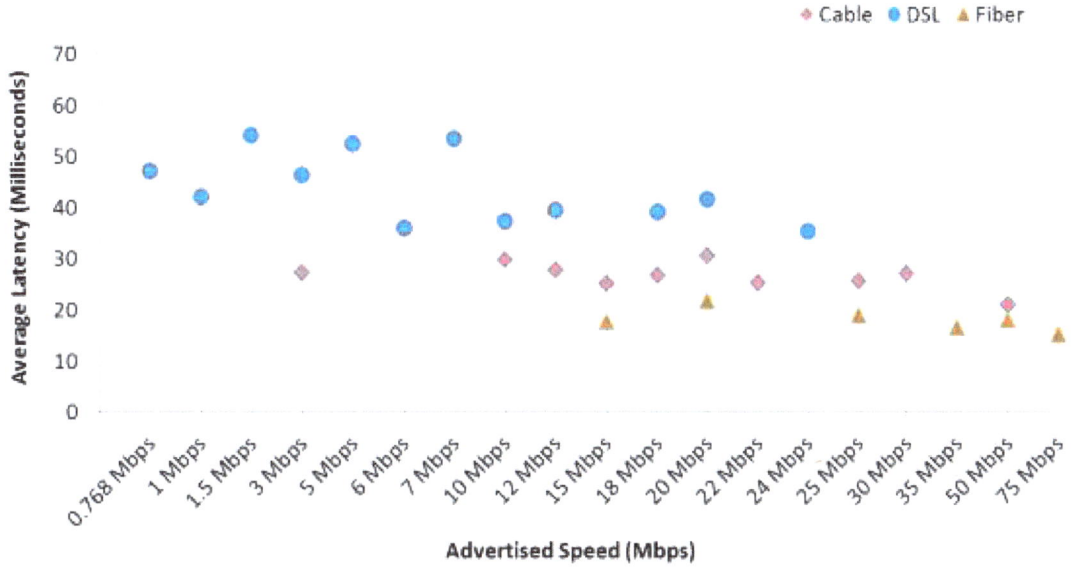

Charts 11.1-11.5 display average web page loading[51] time by speed tier for the September 2012 Test Data. Web pages load much faster as broadband speed increases, but beyond 10 Mbps, performance increases for basic web browsing lessen dramatically. There also appear to be differences in web loading times by service provider at these higher speeds. The data indicate that a consumer subscribing to a 10 Mbps speed tier is unlikely to experience a significant performance increase in basic web browsing—*i.e.*, accessing web pages, but not streaming video or using other high-bandwidth applications such as video chat—by moving to a higher speed tier. These results are largely consistent with and show no significant improvement over previous results. Web page download speeds at higher rates are limited by intrinsic factors (e.g., service architectures, latency, application server speeds, and protocol effects) and not easily improved at the current time. Note that in Charts 11.1-11.5, lower bars indicate shorter load time, and therefore better performance.

Chart 12 shows in a consistent scale across all speed tiers the effect of increasing speed on web loading time. As can be seen in this chart, as speed first increases, there is a steep drop in web loading times, which levels off at about 10 Mbps when the decreasing rate in web page loading time diminishes.

Chart 11.1: Web Loading Time by Advertised Speed, by Technology (1-3 Mbps Tier)—September 2012 Test Data

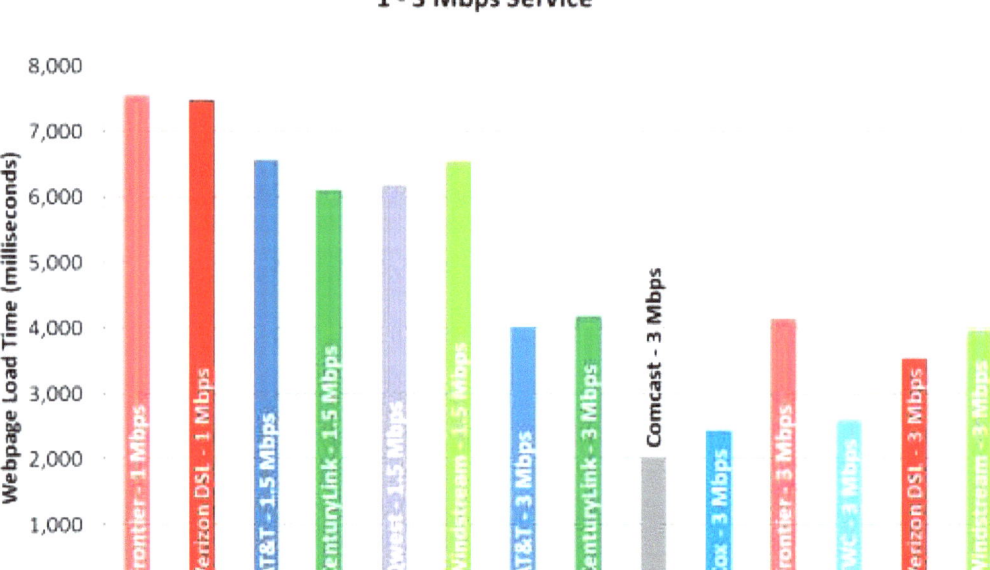

Chart 11.2: Web Loading Time by Advertised Speed, by Technology (5-10 Mbps Tier)—September 2012 Test Data

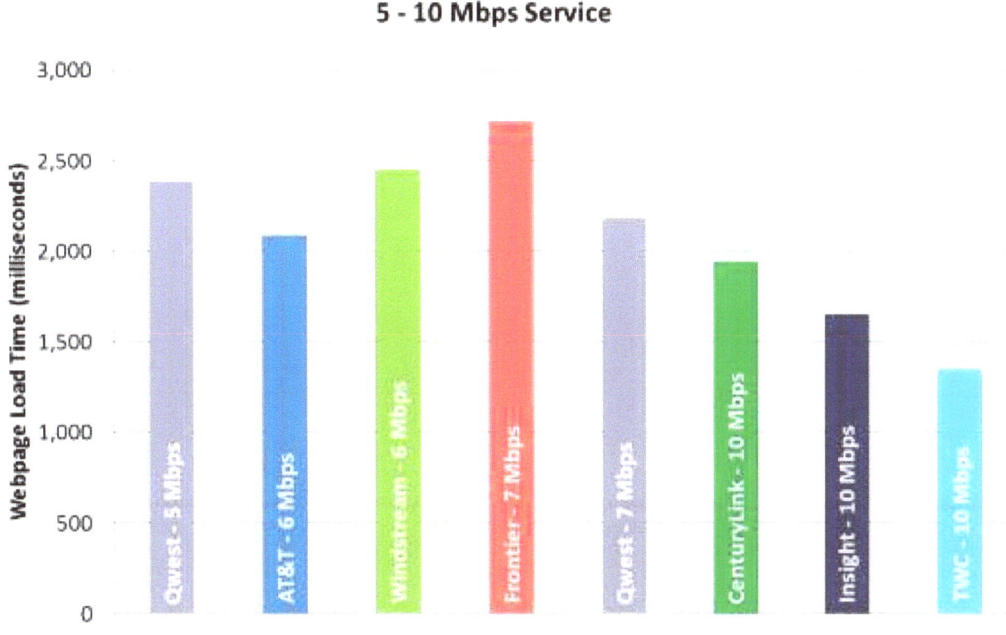

Chart 11.3: Web Loading Time by Advertised Speed, by Technology (12-15 Mbps Tier)—September 2012 Test Data

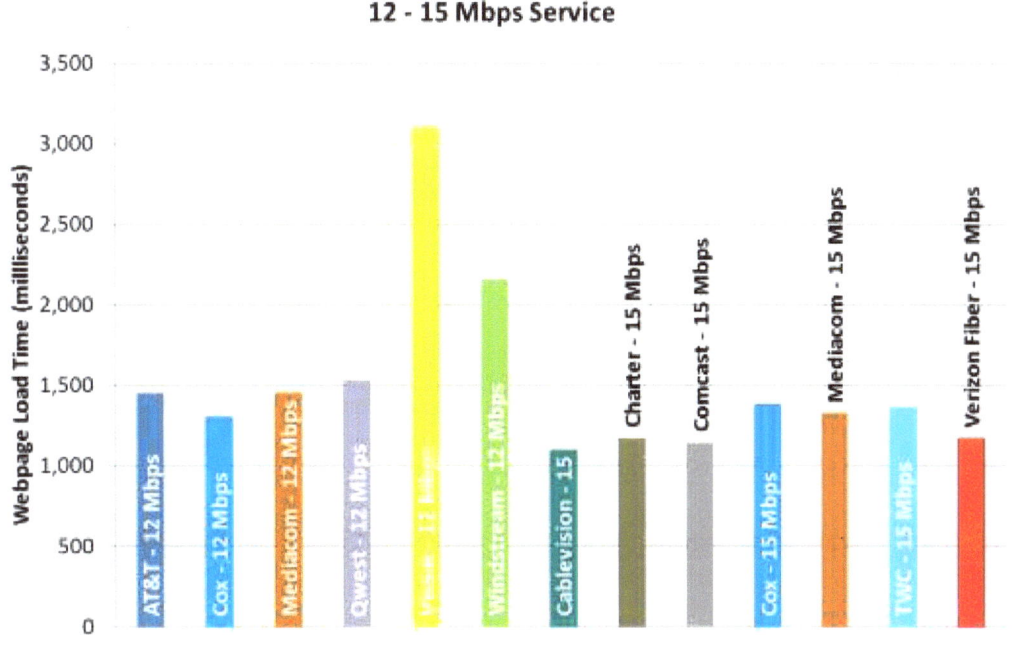

Chart 11.4: Web Loading Time by Advertised Speed, by Technology (18-25 Mbps Tier)—September 2012 Test
Data

Chart 11.5: Web Loading Time by Advertised Speed, by Technology (30-75 Mbps Tier)—September 2012 Test Data

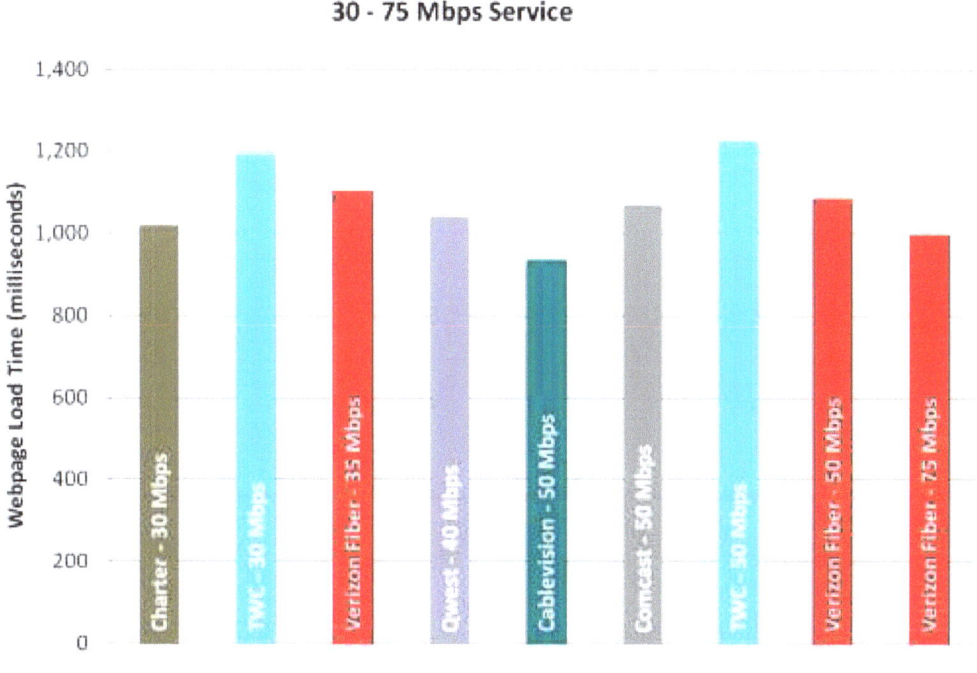

Chart 12: Web Loading Time by Advertised Speed (1-75 Mbps Tier)—September 2012 Test Data

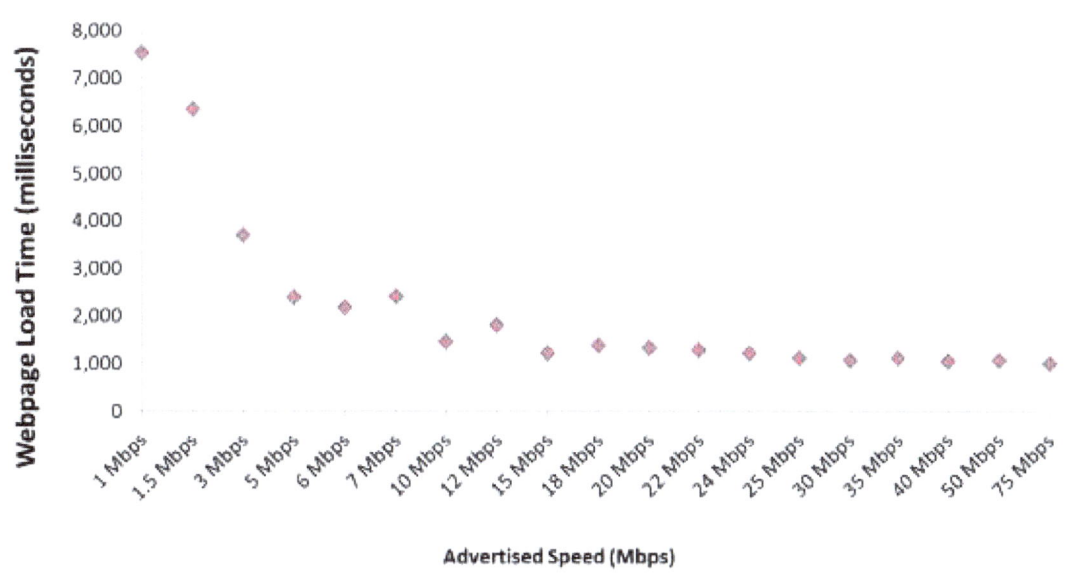

VARIATION BY TIME OF DAY IN DELIVERY OF ADVERTISED SPEED

Chart 13 shows that during the September 2012 testing period, performance during the day varied for most technologies. During idle periods there was more capacity available for the consumer, while at peak usage periods, with many consumers online, available capacity per consumer diminished. As noted earlier in this Report, since the initiation of this measuring program the participating ISPs, on average, have both improved performance and have provided more reliable estimates of actual speeds to consumers. As a result, overall ISP performance has become increasingly consistent.

Chart 13: Hourly Sustained Download Speeds as a Percentage of Advertised, by Provider—September 2012 Test Data

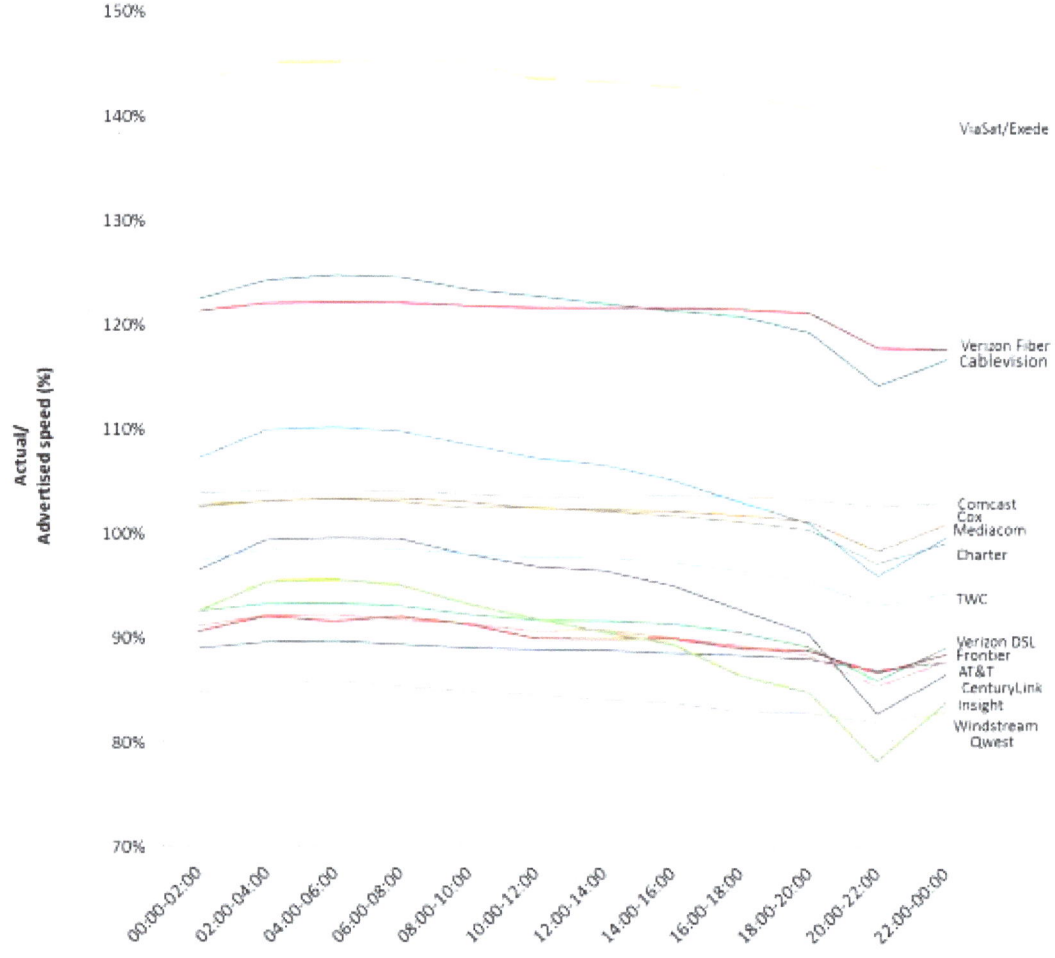

24 HOUR VERSUS PEAK PERFORMANCE VARIATION BY TECHNOLOGY

Chart 14 compares the average hour-by-hour download speed performance for fiber, cable, DSL, and satellite technologies to the 24-hour average speed for each technology. Performance of all technologies fluctuates slightly during the day. For example, while cable technology has a daily 24-hour average speed of slightly over 100 percent of advertised rates, it achieves this by delivering slightly higher than average performance during non-peak hours and slightly lower performance during peak periods.

Chart 14: Average Sustained Download Speeds as a Percentage of Advertised Over a 24-Hour Period, by Technology—September 2012 Test Data

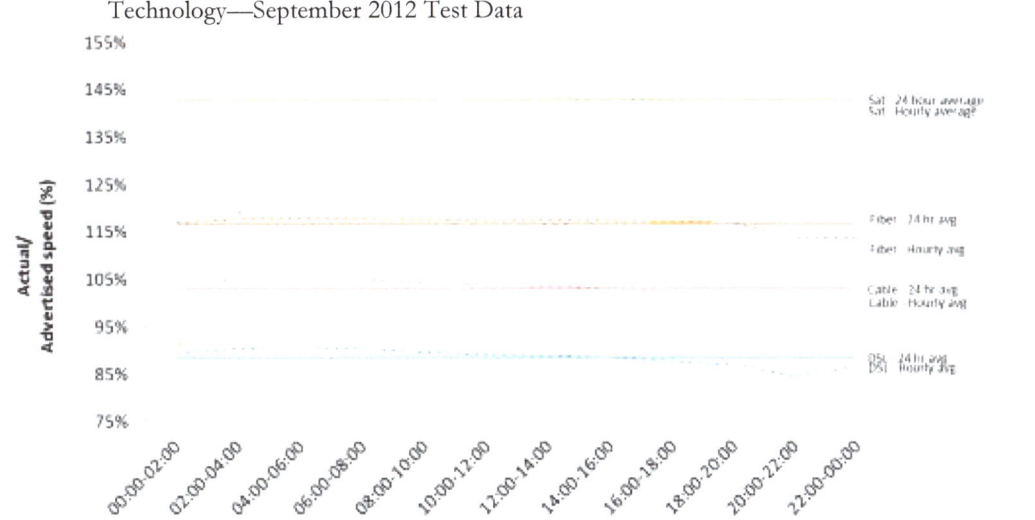

CUMULATIVE DISTRIBUTION FOR DOWNLOAD SPEEDS

As in the last Report, we include cumulative distribution charts to provide some illustration of how broadband performance varies within the sample population. In theory, test results for a particular ISP could return an average performance level that was achieved with an extreme variance in the population. For example, an ISP that delivered well over 100 percent of advertised speed to some subscribers might deliver well under 100 percent of advertised speed to other subscribers and still deliver, on average, 100 percent of advertised speed. The cumulative distribution accounts for this by showing the percent of subscribers to a particular speed tier who experience an average or greater level of performance. For example, if the 90th percentile of the chart intersected with 80 percent of advertised speed, it would indicate that 90 percent of the population is receiving performance of 80 percent or better of advertised speed and that the remaining 10 percent of the population is receiving performance less than 80 percent of advertised speed. We believe that the cumulative distribution charts below provide some reassurance that extreme variance is not resulting in misleading averages. In other words, the average performance numbers used elsewhere in this Report should do a good job of indicating the likely performance for any individual user of a particular ISP and tier. From Chart 15 it can be seen that in the September 2012 testing period at the 80th percentile fiber consumers are receiving 102 percent or better of advertised rates, cable consumers are receiving 98 percent or better, satellite consumers 143 percent of advertised rates, and DSL consumers are receiving 83 percent or better of advertised rates. At the 90th percentile, fiber consumers are receiving 99 percent or better of advertised rates, cable consumers are receiving 95 percent, satellite 140 percent, and DSL consumers 73 percent of advertised rates. It is worth noting that unlike fiber or cable technologies, DSL performance decreases with the length of the cable connecting the DSL subscriber to a broadband aggregation point maintained by the service provider. Thus, DSL subscriber performance will vary as their wire distances vary from this aggregation point.

Chart 15: Cumulative Distribution of Sustained Download Speeds as a Percentage of Advertised Speed, by Technology—September 2012 Test Data

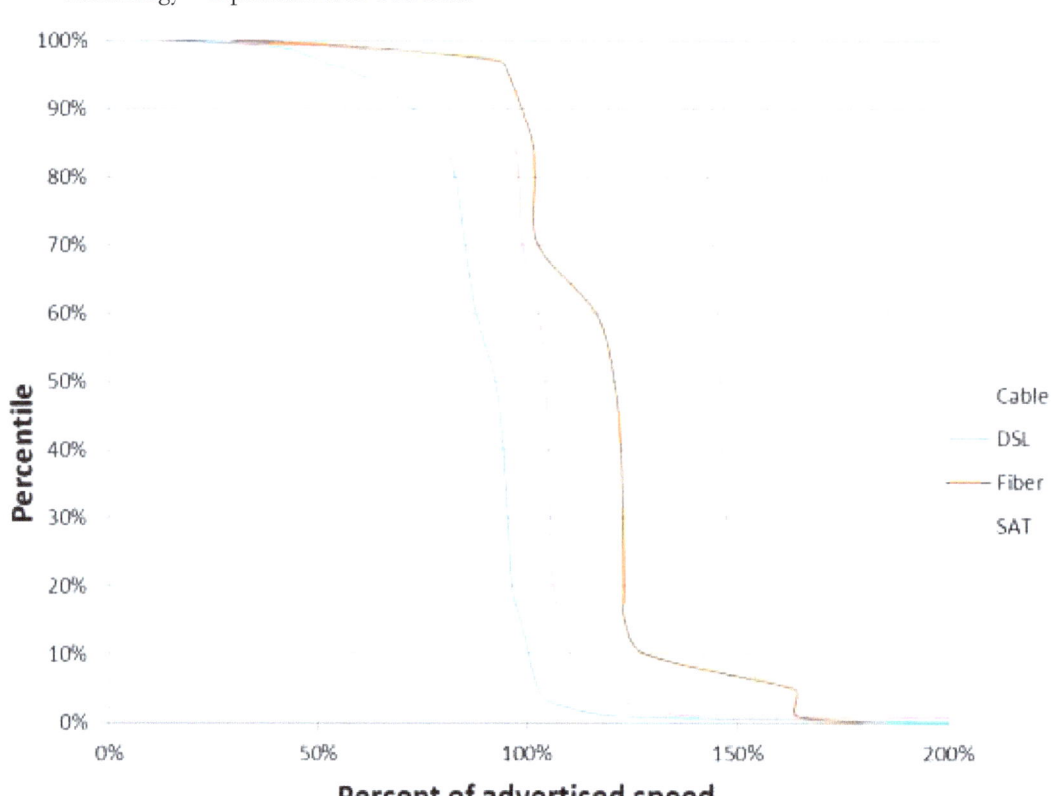

Charts 16.1-16.2 show the cumulative distribution of sustained download speeds by provider. To clarify the data, we have divided the performance of the fifteen ISPs into two charts, with the providers divided into alphabetical order.

Chart 16.1: Cumulative Distribution of Sustained Download Speeds as a Percentage of Advertised Speed, by Provider (7 Providers)—September 2012 Test Data

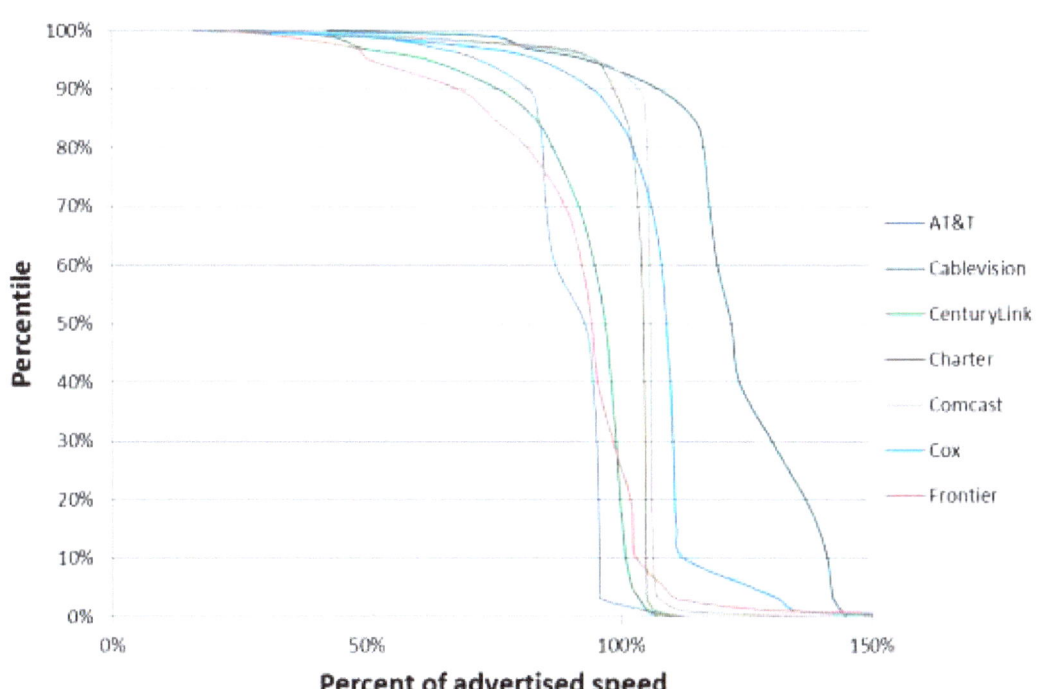

Chart 16.2: Cumulative Distribution of Sustained Download Speeds as a Percentage of Advertised Speed, by Provider (8 providers)—September 2012 Test Data

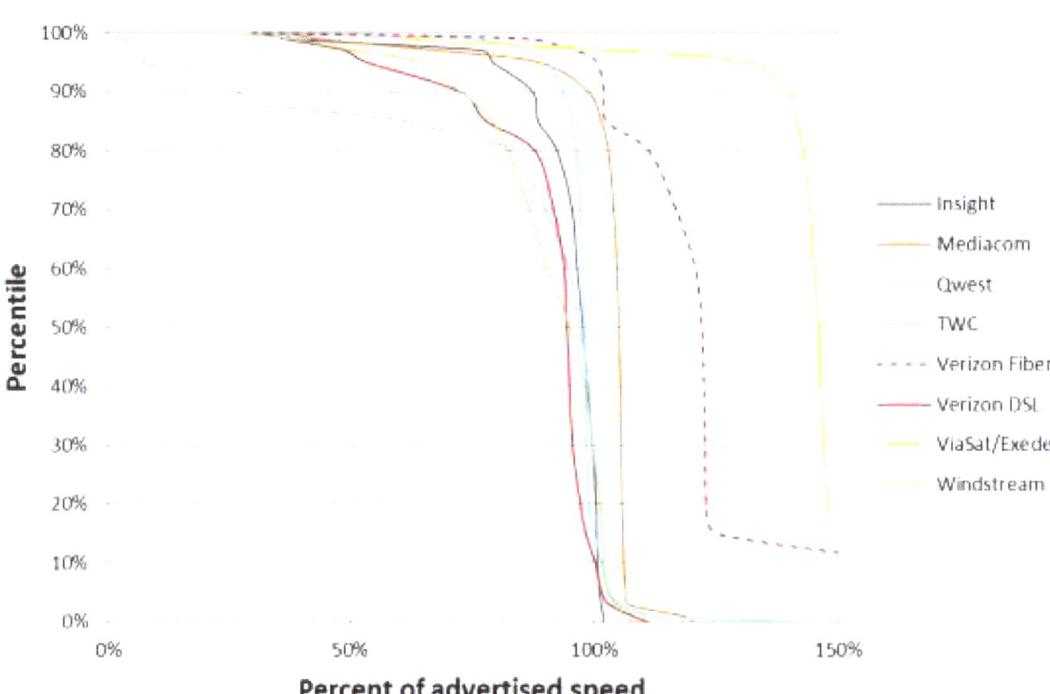

For easier readability, we have also included the CDF data illustrated in Charts 16.1-16.2 as Figure 1.

Figure 1: Cumulative Distribution Percentiles for Sustained Download Speeds as a Percentage of Advertised Speed, by Provider

	20%	50%	70%	80%	90%	95%
AT&T	96%	93%	85%	85%	82%	72%
Cablevision	137%	122%	117%	116%	107%	94%
CenturyLink	100%	97%	92%	87%	76%	62%
Charter	105%	104%	103%	102%	99%	95%
Comcast	106%	106%	105%	105%	104%	96%
Cox	111%	109%	106%	102%	94%	84%
Frontier	102%	94%	89%	82%	68%	51%
Insight	100%	98%	96%	93%	88%	79%
Mediacom	106%	105%	104%	103%	99%	89%
Qwest	93%	86%	83%	81%	70%	60%

TWC	99%	98%	97%	96%	94%	91%
Verizon Fiber	123%	122%	117%	111%	102%	101%
Verizon DSL	97%	95%	92%	88%	73%	53%
ViaSat/Exede	148%	146%	144%	143%	140%	131%
Windstream	101%	95%	87%	82%	73%	64%

CUMULATIVE DISTRIBUTION FOR UPLOAD SPEEDS

As with the cumulative distribution charts for download speeds, Chart 17 shows the percent of subscribers to a particular speed tier who experienced an average or greater level of upload performance in the September 2012 testing period, while Charts 18.1-18.2 show the same results by provider, with the results again split into two charts alphabetically for legibility. These results suggest that DSL, cable, fiber, and satellite return even higher performance, with fewer outliers, for upload than for download speeds.

Chart 17: Cumulative Distribution of Sustained Upload Speeds as a Percentage of Advertised Speed, by Technology—September 2012 Test Data

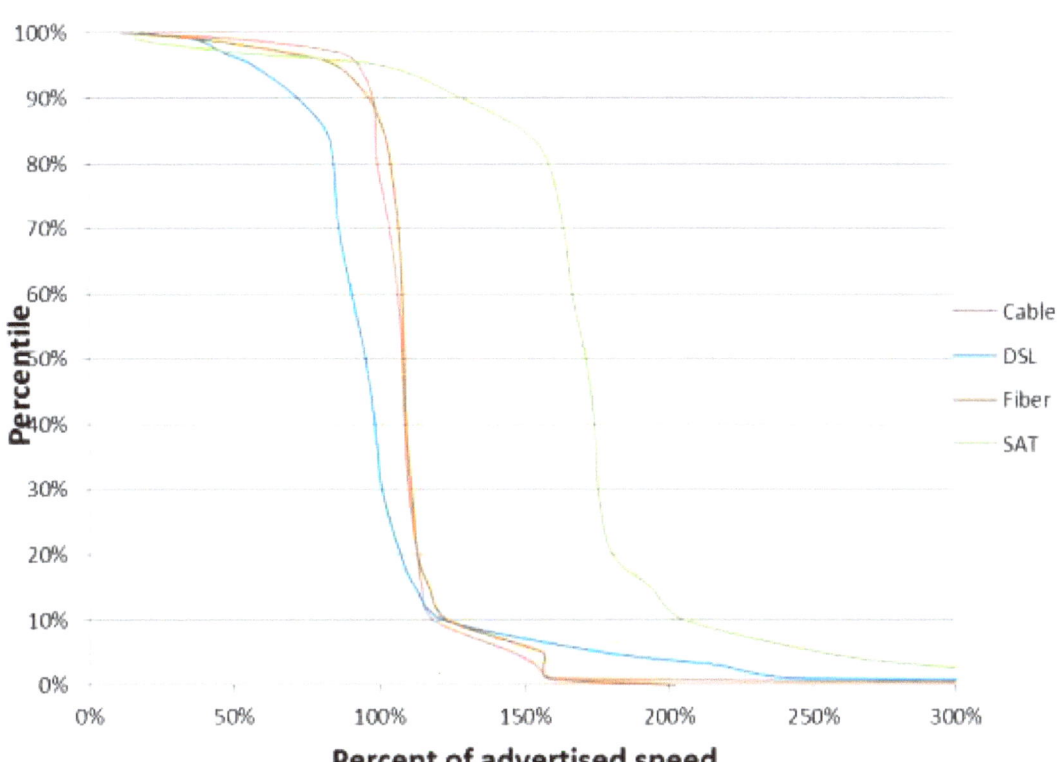

Chart 18.1: Cumulative Distribution of Sustained Upload Speeds as a Percentage of Advertised Speed, by Provider (7 Providers)—September 2012 Test Data

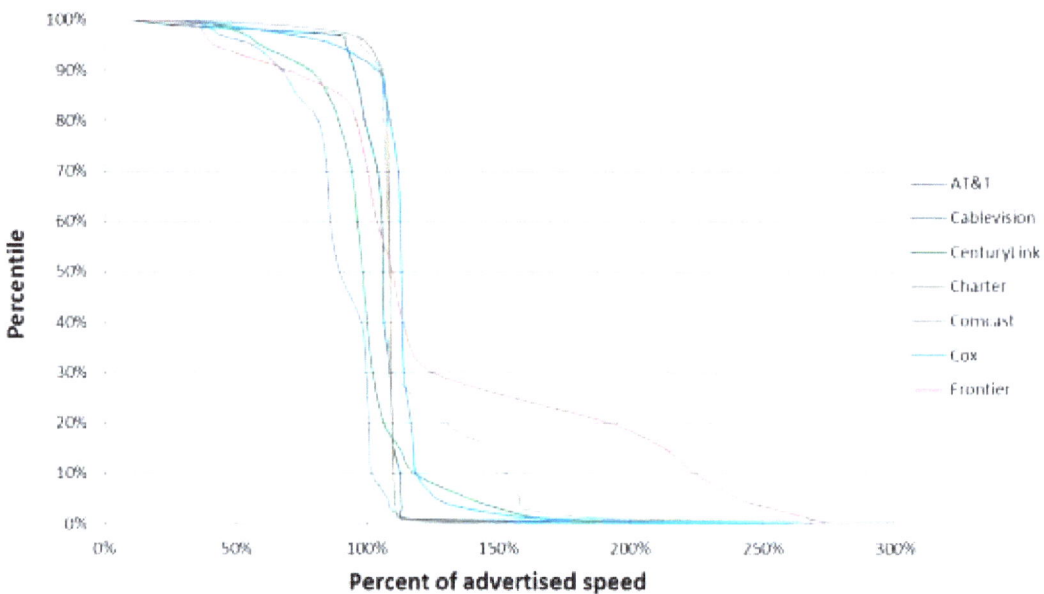

Chart 18.2: Cumulative Distribution of Sustained Upload Speeds as a Percentage of Advertised Speed, by Provider (8 Providers)—September 2012 Test Data

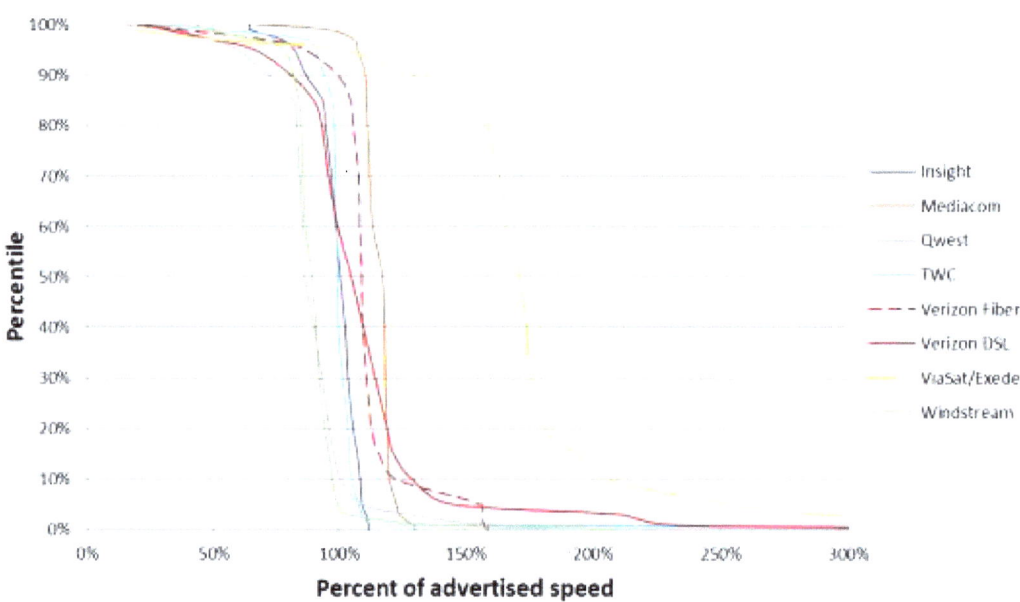

COMPARISON TO LAST REPORTING PERIOD

Figure 2 shows a comparison between April 2012 and September 2012 test data for peak period average download speeds as a percentage of advertised speed. Results closely match the last report.

Figure 2: Comparison of Sustained Actual Download Speed as a Percentage of Advertised Speed (April/September 2012)

ISP	April 2012	September 2012	% Change
AT&T	87%	87%	0%
Cablevision	120%	115%	-4%
CenturyLink	90%	87%	-2%
Charter	98%	98%	0%
Comcast	103%	103%	0%
Cox	95%	97%	3%
Frontier	77%	87%	13%
Insight	92%	85%	-7%
Mediacom	100%	99%	-1%
Qwest	82%	82%	0%
TWC	95%	94%	-2%
Verizon (Fiber)	120%	118%	-2%
Verizon (DSL)	86%	88%	2%
ViaSat/Exede	Not offered	137%	N/A
Windstream	84%	81%	-4%

ACTUAL VERSUS ADVERTISED SPEEDS

Figure 3 below lists the advertised speed tiers included in this study, and compares this with the actual average peak performance results from September 2012. As before, we note that the actual sustained download speeds here were based on national averages, and should not be taken to represent the performance experienced by any one consumer in any specific market for these ISPs.

Figure 3: Peak Period Sustained Download Performance, by Provider—September 2012 Test Data

Actual Sustained Download Speed (Mbps)	Advertised Download Speed Tier (Mbps)	Provider	Actual Sustained Speed / Advertised Speed Tier
0.93	1 Mbps	Verizon (DSL)	93%
0.99	1 Mbps	Frontier	99%
1.17	1.5 Mbps	Windstream	78%
1.21	1.5 Mbps	Qwest	81%
1.27	1.5 Mbps	AT&T	84%
1.35	1.5 Mbps	CenturyLink	90%
2.5	3 Mbps	AT&T	83%
2.51	3 Mbps	Frontier	84%
2.53	3 Mbps	Windstream	84%
2.54	3 Mbps	CenturyLink	85%
2.55	3 Mbps	Verizon (DSL)	85%
2.86	3 Mbps	TWC	95%
3.07	3 Mbps	Comcast	102%
3.17	3 Mbps	Cox	106%
4.47	5 Mbps	Qwest	89%
4.96	6 Mbps	Windstream	83%
5.16	7 Mbps	Frontier	74%
5.2	6 Mbps	AT&T	87%
5.63	7 Mbps	Qwest	80%
8.61	12 Mbps	Windstream	72%
8.76	10 Mbps	CenturyLink	88%
8.97	10 Mbps	Insight	90%
9.48	10 Mbps	TWC	95%
10.1	12 Mbps	Qwest	84%
10.88	12 Mbps	AT&T	91%

Actual Sustained Download Speed (Mbps)	Advertised Download Speed Tier (Mbps)	Provider	Actual Sustained Speed / Advertised Speed Tier
11.86	12 Mbps	Mediacom	99%
13.36	12 Mbps	Cox	111%
13.93	15 Mbps	TWC	93%
14.32	15 Mbps	Cox	95%
14.7	15 Mbps	Charter	98%
15.11	15 Mbps	Mediacom	101%
15.51	15 Mbps	Comcast	103%
15.84	20 Mbps	Insight	79%
16	20 Mbps	Qwest	80%
16.46	18 Mbps	AT&T	91%
16.46	12Mbps	ViaSat/Exede	137%
17.05	18 Mbps	Cox	95%
17.75	20 Mbps	TWC	89%
17.88	15 Mbps	Cablevision	119%
19.41	20 Mbps	Frontier	97%
20.23	15 Mbps	Verizon (Fiber)	135%
20.9	22 Mbps	Cox	95%
21.9	24 Mbps	AT&T	91%
22.88	20 Mbps	Verizon (Fiber)	114%
24.63	25 Mbps	Cox	99%
25.02	25 Mbps	Frontier	100%
25.85	25 Mbps	Comcast	103%
28.05	30 Mbps	TWC	93%
29.02	25 Mbps	Verizon (Fiber)	116%
29.4	30 Mbps	Charter	98%
33.43	40 Mbps	Qwest	84%
40.78	35 Mbps	Verizon (Fiber)	117%
47.48	50 Mbps	TWC	95%

Actual Sustained Download Speed (Mbps)	Advertised Download Speed Tier (Mbps)	Provider	Actual Sustained Speed / Advertised Speed Tier
48.52	50 Mbps	Comcast	97%
52.55	50 Mbps	Cablevision	105%
55.28	50 Mbps	Verizon (Fiber)	111%
77.58	75 Mbps	Verizon (Fiber)	103%

DATA CONSUMPTION

Test traffic data use is tracked and subtracted from each consumer panelist's personal data usage, which allows us to include a chart demonstrating consumer data consumption. The September 2012 data was taken from a subset of 5046 measurement devices that were active during the measurement period,[52] that reported a total of 301 terabytes[53] of data consumed, which represents the amount of data uploaded and downloaded through all measurement devices across the panel, minus traffic associated with the execution of Measuring Broadband America performance measurements. Chart 19 shows the average amount of data traffic consumed by users in each speed tier normalized as a percentage of total traffic generated by all consumers.[54] In effect, we compute the ratio of the mean measurement device consumption rate for a specific tier and the mean measurement device consumption rate across all tiers. This normalized view of user traffic shows a correlation between data consumption and speed tiers. In general, we found a correlation between higher speed tiers and greater data consumption by the average user. This could mean that as higher speeds are made available to consumers, consumers increase the amount of data they consume, through some combination of greater use of the Internet and adoption of more data-intensive applications and services; or that consumers who use higher data-intensive applications on the Internet tend to subscribe to faster speed tiers.

Chart 20 shows the cumulative distribution function of traffic by technology demonstrating how much traffic was consumed by different percentages of users. One important note about the data consumption information presented in this Report: The panel methodology specifically attempted to exclude both users with high consumption profiles and very fast tiers that had relatively low subscription rates. For these and other reasons, while the data do show a correlation between speed tier and data consumption, no conclusions can be drawn about total data consumption by broadband subscribers. In other words, while Chart 20 does not show data consumption above roughly 160 GB, that does not mean that typical broadband subscribers do not consume more than that amount each month, just that such subscribers would be excluded by the methodology of the Report. In addition, data consumption within the sample population has increased from the previous study.

Satellite is a new addition to Chart 20. The satellite business model does not support large data caps, and this is evident in the behaviour of the satellite consumers who participated in the study.[55]

Chart 19: Normalized Average User Traffic—September 2012 Test Data

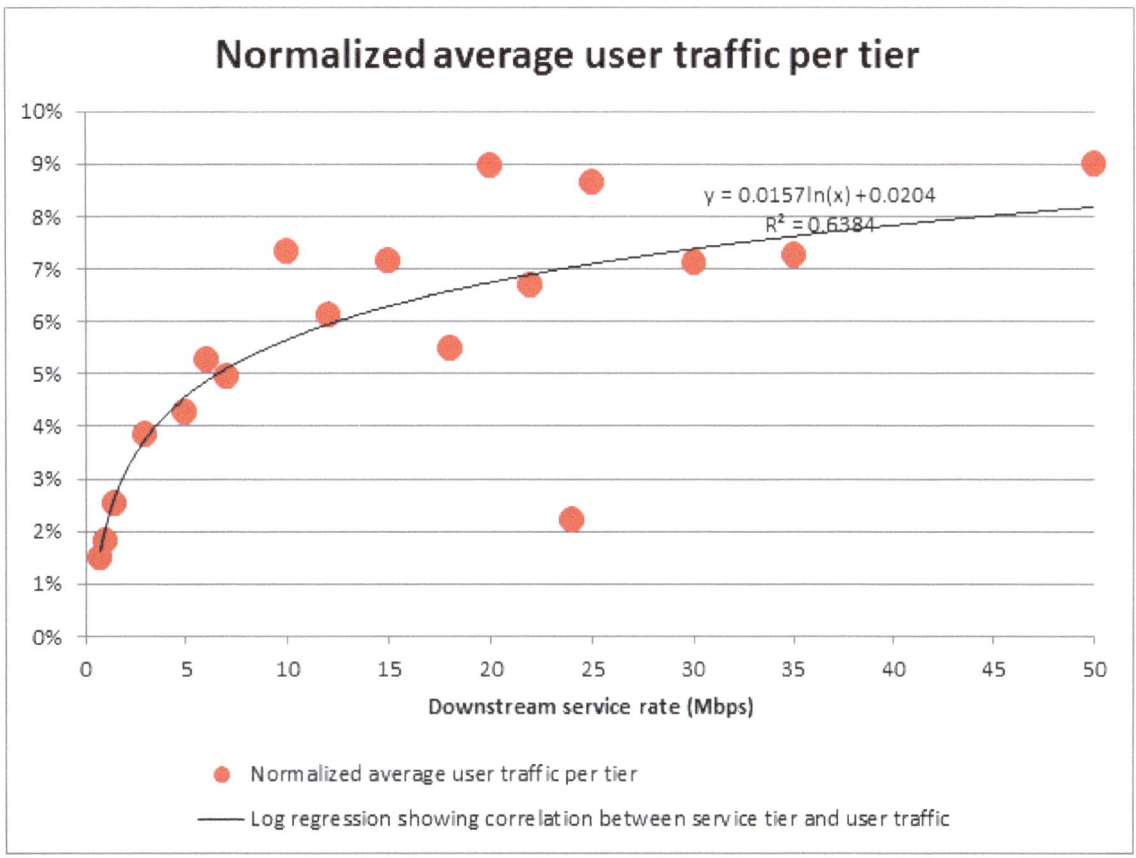

Chart 20: Cumulative Distribution of User Traffic, by Technology—September 2012 Test Data

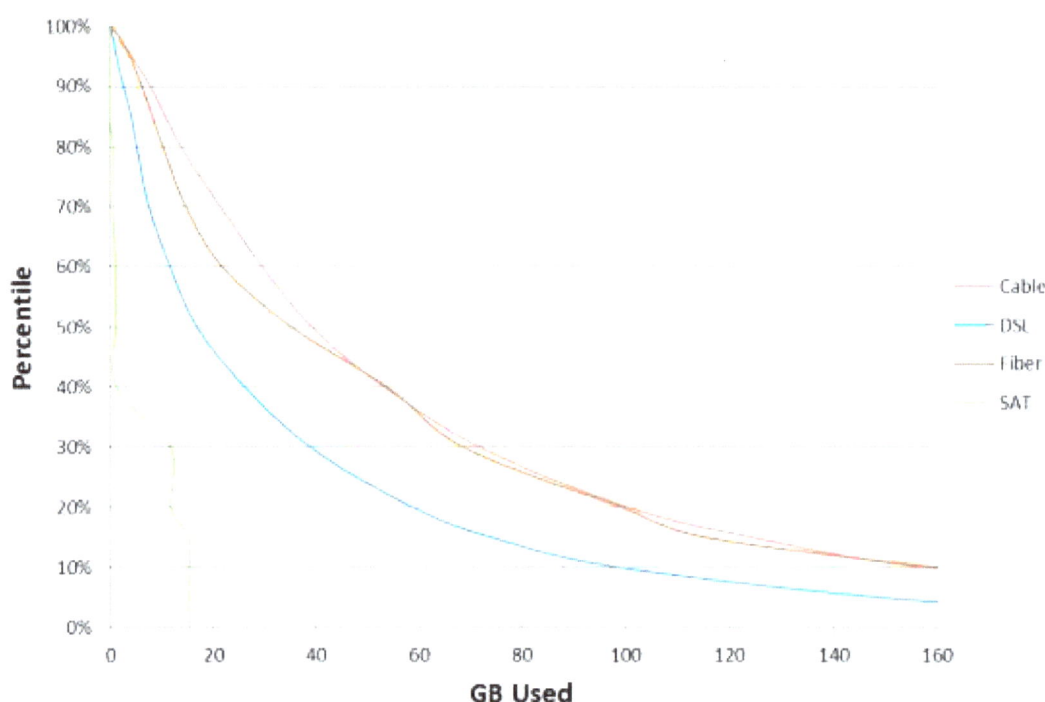

PANELIST MIGRATION

From the April 2012 study, 6,635 panelists continued to participate and to report data in September 2012.[56] Figure 4 provides a percentage comparison of the 1,171 panelists who were part of the April 2012 study and migrated to a different speed tier between the April 2012 and September 2012 data collection periods. This table only includes panelists who were in both the April 2012 and September 2012 study. The highlighted boxes show the percentage of panelists who stayed in each tier from April 2012 to September 2012; the boxes to the left and right of those highlighted represent panelists who decreased or increased their speed, respectively, during this period.

Figure 4: Comparison of Panelist Population by Speed Tier—April 2012 and September 2012 Test Data

April 2012 Range	September 2012 Range									
	0-1	1-3	3-7	7-10	10-15	15-20	20-25	25-30	30-50	50+
0-1	53.7%	21.1%	9.5%	1.1%	9.5%	2.1%	1.1%	0.0%	1.1%	1.1%
1-3	1.5%	77.7%	14.2%	0.5%	4.3%	1.0%	0.0%	0.5%	0.0%	0.3%
3-7	0.5%	3.8%	84.8%	1.9%	4.2%	3.0%	0.4%	0.2%	0.5%	0.6%
7-10	0.4%	1.3%	10.0%	61.5%	10.0%	15.5%	0.4%	0.4%	0.0%	0.4%
10-15	0.0%	0.3%	1.2%	0.2%	88.4%	5.5%	3.1%	0.3%	0.9%	0.2%
15-20	0.1%	0.0%	1.0%	0.1%	2.7%	86.0%	3.5%	2.3%	3.3%	1.0%
20-25	0.0%	0.5%	0.5%	0.2%	1.7%	12.8%	73.4%	4.4%	2.7%	3.9%
25-30	0.0%	0.0%	0.3%	0.0%	0.5%	6.7%	1.2%	71.8%	4.0%	15.5%
30-50	0.0%	0.0%	0.6%	0.2%	0.2%	2.5%	0.8%	0.6%	84.3%	10.9%
50+	0.0%	0.0%	0.8%	0.0%	0.8%	1.5%	1.5%	3.8%	0.8%	90.8%

As indicated earlier, panelists in September 2012 were, on average, subscribing to higher speed tiers than were panelists in April 2012. Chart 21 shows the percent of April panelists that were subscribed to a higher tier in September 2012. The bars indicate the percentage of panelists from each of the April 2012 tiers that had moved to a higher tier by the September 2012 testing period. The largest increases can be observed in the 0-1 Mbps, 1-3 Mbps, 7-10 Mbps, and 25-30 Mbps tiers where providers have made company-wide upgrades to subscriber tiers.[57] The tiers that panelists in the April 2012 study moved to in September 2012 are shown in Chart 22, and demonstrate that many subscribers moved to a tier in the next higher band.

Chart 21: Percent Change of April 2012 Panelists Subscribed to Higher Tier in September 2012

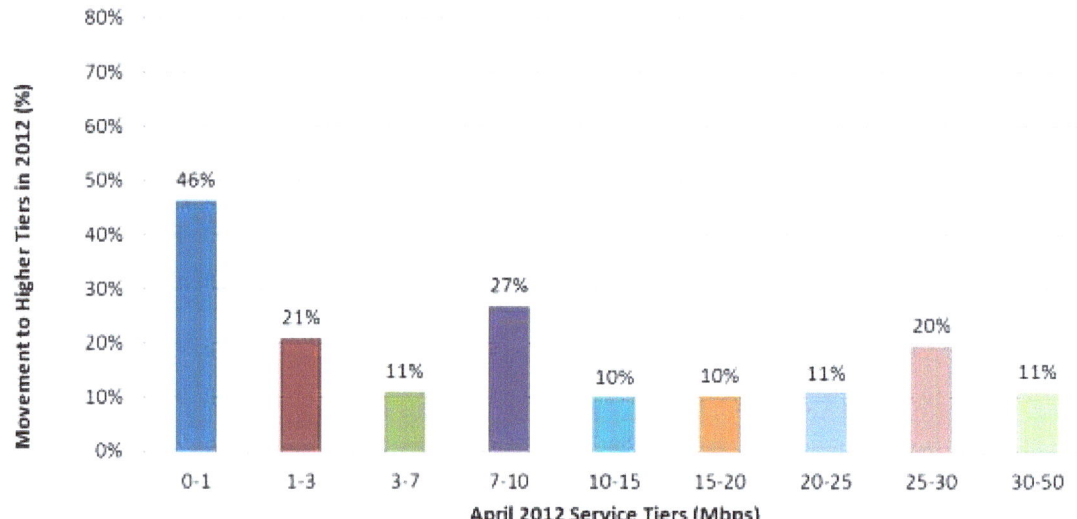

Chart 22: Percent Change of April 2012 Panelists Subscribed to Higher Tier in September 2012

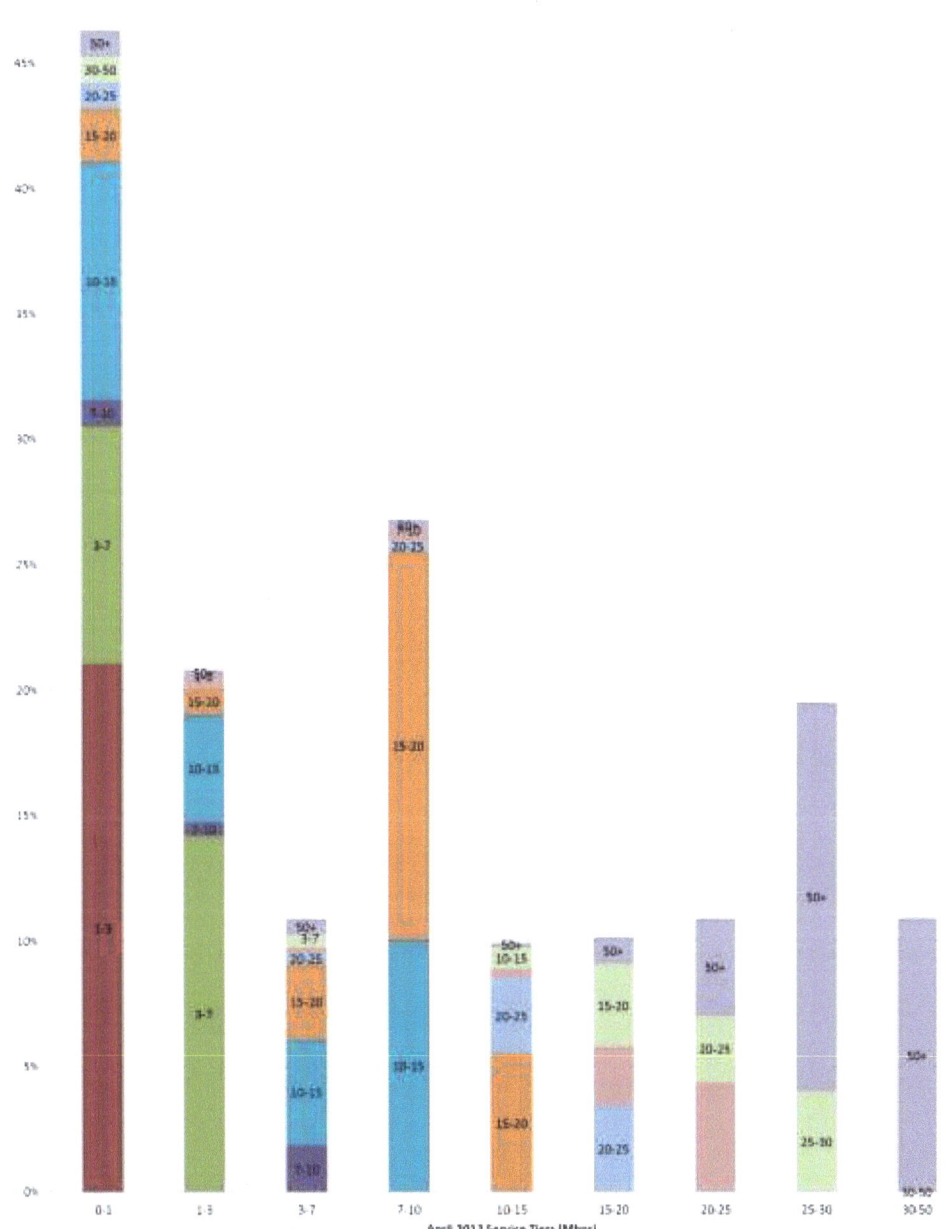

April 2012 Service Tiers (Mbps)

Conclusion and Next Steps

The relatively short time span between this Report and the July 2012 Report allowed us to confirm many of the findings from that previous study. Consumers are continuing to show the importance of higher speed tiers for their needs by migrating their service plans to those tiers. Some of our results suggest that while consumers receive an immediate benefit from higher speeds, improvements in the overall Internet ecosystem may be necessary to fully realize the benefits of very high speeds.

The future of the Measuring Broadband America program

Following recommendations included in the National Broadband Plan, the FCC remains committed to working with industry groups to develop awareness of broadband performance in an open and transparent environment. During 2013 we expect to implement another one-month testing period for fixed broadband, and to release an update to this report. In addition, we plan to conduct testing on mobile broadband performance, and will release a separate report on Measuring Broadband America in the mobile environment, which will again be produced in cooperation with major industry participants, academics, and stakeholders. The collaborative work that has produced these reports has also resulted in ongoing discussions with industry and others on best practices for collecting broadband performance data, as well as on how best to report this data.

This Report, like the reports that preceded it, could not have been produced without the benefit of the ongoing discussions held with a broad array of individuals and entities, including the participating ISPs, equipment manufacturers, M-Lab,[58] and academics.

Broadband Testing Program

The next testing period for this program is scheduled for September 2013, one year from the testing period analyzed in this Report. Over the next year, we anticipate that providers will continue to innovate and increase their offerings in the higher speed tiers. We know based on industry discussions that the major expansion in high speed service tiers first noted in the July 2012 report was enabled by the deployment by the cable industry of DOCSIS 3.0 technology which permitted service rates of 100 Mbps and above. The cable industry has also announced that it intends in the near future to extend its services to rates beyond 100 Mbps, both to support future service offerings such as ultra-high definition television,[59] and to meet competition created by fiber-based service providers. Verizon fiber is now offering rates up to 300 Mbps in select parts of their market footprint, while Google offers 1 Gbps (1000 Mbps) service in Kansas City, MO.

We recognize that the transition to higher speeds will not be without challenges. Changes in offerings from edge innovators, equipment manufacturers, as well as consumers' use of broadband applications and services may be required to take full advantage of these higher rates. Regardless, our test results have consistently illustrated that subscribers to higher speed tiers generally use more data than other consumers and thus are immediately benefitting from these higher rates. We remain confident that industry will meet the challenge of responding to consumer demand for speed, and data capacity, and that both of these measures will continue to grow in the years to come.

While this Report already provides information relevant to the vast majority of broadband subscribers in the U.S., we have plans to significantly expand the Measuring Broadband America program. In addition to continuing the existing program, we plan to test and deliver information about additional broadband delivery technologies, including mobile broadband, to more comprehensively detail the consumer broadband experience. We are also working with our industry partners to discuss more specialized studies that we believe will help to identify other areas of broadband network performance that impact the overall consumer experience. We hope to produce one or more such specialized reports in 2013.

Launch of Measuring Broadband America: Mobile

After extensive discussions with the mobile broadband industry, including the major service providers as well as CTIA, the industry's trade association, we have committed to undertaking the first comprehensive public study of mobile broadband performance in the United States. Drawing on our experience with public/private partnerships in the fixed Measuring Broadband America program, in 2012 the FCC invited and received support from leading wireless carriers and the major industry trade associations to help develop a program to study mobile broadband performance in the U.S. in an open and transparent manner. Due to the dynamic nature of mobile performance, this is a more complex undertaking than our fixed broadband measurement efforts and we expect the mobile efforts to evolve over time with increased knowledge and with ongoing industry discussion. We are grateful for the support we have received from industry in undertaking this effort. As in our previous efforts in the fixed broadband program, we believe working in partnership with key industry participants provides a better understanding of the challenges in developing a measurement program and results in a better product delivered to the consumer.

Measuring mobile broadband performance presents different technical challenges than fixed, and we are adapting our technology to these challenges. Consumers who volunteer for the program will download an application onto their smartphones, which will serve the same function that the Whitebox had in the fixed effort. As it is easier to download an application than install a Whitebox, we expect to be able to welcome more volunteers, and gather data with a much higher resolution, which has the potential to permit the mapping of service areas and speeds, as well as to highlight mobile broadband dead zones.

Testing of Additional Technologies

This report marked the first time we have presented test data on satellite-based broadband. Although ViaSat/Exede is the first service provider to launch this new generation of technology, it is not the only satellite-based ISP committed to implementing improvements to this technology. We hope in future reports to include test results from additional broadband satellite service providers.

Expanding Program to Include Targeted Studies of Specific Performance Metrics

As discussed in this report, Measuring Broadband America was initially focused on measuring broadband performance from the consumer to the end of the service provider's network. This simplified our initial task, as also aligned with the service offerings provided by ISPs to consumers. However, Internet services and applications are supported by an end-to-end connection linking the application or service provider to the consumer in a complex and variable arrangement of network interconnections. A consumer may literally span the globe in browsing the website of a company, news service or government website. Working with our partners on this project, we will be seeking other ways to better leverage our measurement system and provide better information to consumers and more insights into the evolving performance of the Internet.

Commitment to Transparency

Both the Commission and SamKnows recognize that while the methodology descriptions included in this document provide an overview of the project as a whole, there will be experts, as well as members of the public and non-profit organizations, who are willing to contribute to the project by reviewing the actual software used in the testing. SamKnows welcomes review of its software and technical platform for non-commercial purposes only.

All Data Released into the Public Domain

In the interest of transparency and to support additional research, the full Raw Bulk Data Set acquired during this study will be made available to the public.[60]

Acknowledgements

This Report benefited from the voluntary participation of a number of parties. The contribution of their expertise to the development of the methodologies employed in this Report materially increased its quality. We would like to extend our thanks to the following entities:

- Adtran
- AT&T
- Cablevision Systems Corporation
- CenturyLink
- Charter Communications
- Comcast
- Corning
- Cox Communications
- Fiber to the Home Council
- Frontier Communications Company
- Georgia Institute of Technology
- Genband
- Insight Communications
- Intel
- Internet Society
- JDSU
- Mediacom Communications Corporation
- Massachusetts Institute of Technology
- M-Lab
- Motorola
- National Cable & Telecommunications Association
- New America Foundation
- Practicum Team, NCSU, Institute for Advanced Analytics
- Qwest Communications
- Time Warner Cable
- US Telecom Association
- Verizon
- ViaSat
- Windstream Communications

Finally, we again thank SamKnows for their performance during this endeavor, as they remain critical to this study's success.

[1] Throughout this report, observations on satellite technology are based on test results from ViaSat, which retails consumer broadband under the brand name Exede Internet.

[2] See "Next Generation Satellite Broadband Passes Important Test," December 8, 2011, at http://www.telecompetitor.com/next-generation-satellite-broadband-passes-important-test (last accessed February 3, 2013).

[3] The August 2011 Report and its supporting data sets can be accessed at fcc.us/mba0811report; the July 2012 Report and its supporting data sets can be accessed at fcc.us/mba0712report.

[4] In this report we use the terms subscribed speed and advertised speed. The subscribed speed is the nominal service speed associated with a service offered to a consumer. Depending on the service access technology and service provider policies, actual speeds delivered to each consumer may be less than, close to or even exceed a subscribed speed. The subscribed speed is often used in competitive advertisements by the service provider and is commonly called the advertised speed.

[5] As described in more detail below, both the August 2011 Report and the July 2012 Report were based on the results of testing that took place over a one month period, and do not necessarily represent performance over an entire year. In addition, unless otherwise specified, results on increases and decreases in broadband performance are not statistically significant.

[6] Results from these higher service tiers are not included here because they are not yet available to a sufficiently large consumer base to meet our statistical thresholds for inclusion in the study.

[7] Qwest 40 Mbps; Comcast 50 Mbps; Time Warner Cable 50 Mbps; Verizon 50 Mbps; and Verizon Fiber 75 Mbps.

[8] Verizon Fiber 25 Mbps.

[9] See http://www.viasat.com/files/assets/assets/ViaSat-1%20FAQ%201_10%20V5.pdf (last accessed February 13, 2013); "ViaSat-1 and Ka-Sat: Satellite Communications on Steroids," http://bradshaw-vacuum-technology.com/viasat_kasat.htm (last accessed February 3, 2013).

[10] As described more fully in the Technical Appendix, this study initially allowed for a target deployment in up to 10,000 homes across the United States, and the final volunteer pool was created from over 75,000 initial volunteer broadband subscribers.

[11] Verizon's FiOS service, which is included in this report, is one example of an Internet service using optical fiber technology. In contrast, AT&T's U-Verse is a service mark supporting a bundled service package of voice, video, and Internet services which incorporates multiple technologies: the most common arrangement is a fiber-to-the-node architecture with DSL technology terminating to the home. Most U-Verse panelists tested during this survey utilized DSL technology.

[12] Participating ISPs were: AT&T (DSL); Cablevision (cable); CenturyLink (DSL); Charter (cable); Comcast (cable); Cox (cable); Frontier (DSL/fiber); Insight (cable); Mediacom

(cable); Qwest (DSL); TimeWarner Cable (TWC) (cable); Verizon (DSL and fiber-to-the-home); Windstream (DSL); and ViaSat (satellite).

[13] Sustained speeds are described in the Technical Appendix and are averaged over five second intervals across the high and low rates that might dynamically occur in very short time interval measurements.

[14] ISPs typically advertise a small number of speed tiers but must also support legacy tiers that are no longer offered to new customers. As a result, a service provider may be required to support as many as ten service tiers at a given time.

[15] This limitation was a result of the finite number of measurement devices—approximately 10,000—that could be deployed over the course of the project. Region-specific data would have required an order of magnitude or greater deployment of equipment, at a corresponding increase in cost.

[16] In 2012 the FCC and industry representatives jointly submitted proposals on broadband measurement technology to two standards organizations, the Internet Engineering Task Force and the Broadband Forum, and also supported related work by the IEEE Computer Society. The goal of these proposals would ultimately be to standardize broadband measurements as well as methods that would allow the more efficient collection of such data.

[17] These are unweighted averages based on individual white boxes. However, white boxes are distributed across companies based on market share data provided to the FCC by each company on FCC Form 477 and based on direct communication between the FCC and individual companies. As a result, there is a close correlation between these unweighted averages and results that would be weighted by market share.

[18] The term "average" applied to results in this report always means the arithmetic mean of the sample set under consideration. There is no weighting of samples in calculating averages.

[19] A 24-hour average was computed each day and then averaged over Monday through Sunday.

[20] When ViaSat is excluded from this calculation, this decrease becomes 3.6%.

[21] This is an unweighted average across all ISPs.

[22] In this context, the closest server is the measurement server providing minimum round-trip time.

[23] This was calculated by taking an unweighted average of latency for cable, DSL, and fiber from the Latency sheet in the statistical averages test results.

[24] This was calculated by taking the percentage change of the unweighted average cable, DSL, and fiber 24 hour test results and the peak results for the same technologies in the statistical averages test results.

[25] For example, downloading a large file while browsing the web would limit the effectiveness of burst technology.

[26] As discussed later in the Report, due to latency concerns, the situation is more complex for satellite.

[27] See, e.g., guidelines from Netflix support at http://support.netflix.com/en/node/87#gsc.tab=0 (last accessed on January 1, 2013).

[28] Video content delivery companies are currently researching ultra-high definition video services (e.g., 4K technology, which has a resolution of 12 Megapixels per frame, versus present day 1080p High Definition television with a 2 Megapixel resolution), which would require even higher transmission speeds.

[29] Daniel R. Glover, Hans Kruse, TCP Performance in a Geostationary Satellite Environment, Annual Rev. of Comm. 1998, Int'l Eng. Consortium.

[30] With regard to latency, the International Telecommunications Union (ITU) has suggested that one-way latency of less than 150 ms may affect some applications, while latency greater than 400 ms is unacceptable for most uses of a broadband network. See http://www.itu.int/rec/T-REC-G.114/en. For applications such as interactive data or video, the ITU notes that there are no agreed-upon assessment tools, and recommends that delays be monitored on a case-by-case basis. While we found ViaSat to have a measured one-way latency of 314 ms, this was for comparative purposes only and represented latency only within the portion of the network that we test for all ISPs. We would expect end-to-end latency to be somewhat higher than this figure due to a variety of factors.

[31] At the time of launch, this surpassed the total capacity of all satellites serving North America. See "Viasat broadband 'super-satellite' launches" at http://www.bbc.co.uk/news/science-environment-15358121 (last accessed January 30, 2013).

[32] One popular consumer activity, watching video over the Internet, can consume as much as 2.3 GB/hour. See guidelines from Netflix support at http://support.netflix.com/en/node/87#gsc.tab=0 (last accessed January 1, 2013). Thus a single 2 hour movie could comprise 25 to 50 percent of a monthly data cap.

[33] In addition to the various data sets, the actual software code that was used for the testing will be made available for academic and other researchers for non-commercial purposes. To apply for non-commercial review of the code, interested parties may contact SamKnows directly at team@samknows.com, with the subject heading "Academic Code Review."

[34] This data will be available when released through the FCC website at http://www.fcc.gov/measuring-broadband-america.

[35] Actual information throughputs depend upon many factors including transmission speed, transport protocol characteristics, network states as well as the capabilities of equipment sending or receiving information across the network. At higher speeds, the interplay of these factors becomes more evident.

[36] A byte is a standard unit of measure in computing indicating 8 bits. A megabyte represents one million bytes.

[37] Latency is often colloquially called the "ping time," named after a network tool used to measure the latency. The measurement methodology used in this report differs slightly from that tool, but measures the same round trip transit time between two points.

[38] See International Telecommunication Union (ITU), Series G: Transmission Systems and Media, Digital Systems and Networks; International Telephone Connections and Circuits— General Recommendations on the Transmission Quality for an Entire International Telephone Connection, G.114 (May 2003).

[39] As noted earlier, the full results of all 13 tests that were run in September 2012 are available at fcc.us/mba0213testresults.

[40] The September 2012 data set was validated to remove anomalies that would have produced errors in the report. This data validation process is described in the Technical Appendix.

[41] For a discussion of how averages were calculated for the purposes of this report, *see supra* note 18.

[42] Results from a particular company may include different technology platforms (e.g., results for Cox include both their DOCSIS 2.0 and DOCSIS 3.0 cable technologies; results for Verizon include both DSL and fiber). Throughout this Report, results are recorded separately for CenturyLink and Qwest. These two entities completed a merger on April 1, 2011; however, they continue to integrate operations in 2012. Similarly, Insight Communications was acquired by Time Warner Cable on August 13, 2011. To ensure continuity testing in September 2012, we continued to measure subscribers of the formerly distinct ISPs separately. We may revise this policy as these companies continue their merger integration.

[43] For a comparison of April and September 2012 download speeds, see Figure 2, *supra* at 43.

[44] As noted elsewhere, *see supra* note 18, all averages used in this Report are unweighted arithmetic averages of the relevant data sets. However, the sample plan was based on market share data for all ISPs. Comparison of unweighted averages with averages weighted by market share showed close agreement.

[45] 21 out of 59 service tiers tested in this study returned less than 90 percent of advertised performance during peak periods.

[46] A comparison of AT&T upload performance between this report and the previous report identified a discrepancy in the July 2012 Report which showed an upload speed for AT&T at the 3 Mbps service tier of nearly 150 percent. The current report shows an upload speed of 98 percent which we believe to be correct, and more accurate than the figure included in the previous report. The earlier discrepancy was caused by a failure, during the preparation of the July 2012 Report, to identify several consumers who had changed service providers and speed tiers.

[47] The FCC does not have detailed information on which speed tiers employ burst speed technology. This chart shows the percent difference between the sustained speed and bursts speed tests. Large differences in these speeds can be inferred as the result of burst speed technology being employed.

[48] We provide latency figures for peak periods. Latencies measured for other periods can be found in fcc.us/mba0213testresults.

[49] Due to the order of magnitude difference between terrestrial and satellite latencies, for clarity sake we choose not to include satellite latency in Chart 10.

[50] With the exception of ViaSat/Exede, all recorded latencies are well under International Telecommunication Union (ITU) recommendations of a maximum of 150 ms latency.

[51] For a definition of web loading time, *see* Technical Appendix at 23.

[52] For a discussion of the measurement devices used in this study, *see* Technical Appendix at 15-18. Although in throughout the Report we draw from test results from 6,733 panelists reporting in September 2012, some of the Whiteboxes were unable to collect byte count data, and consequently results for only 5,046 Whiteboxes are included in this measure.

[53] 1 terabyte is 1000000000000 bytes or 1000 gigabytes.

[54] The drop off for the 24 Mbps tier reflects the small number of volunteers participating in this study that were subscribed to this tier.

[55] In the 24 Mbps speed tier, there is only one company represented (AT&T).

[56] Prior to the September 2012 testing period, 6,635 panelists from the July 2012 sample continued to supply data via their measurement devices. In addition, 405 subscribers were recruited after the July 2012 testing period, which brought the total subscribers reporting data in September 2012 to 7,040. After the data were processed, as discussed in more detail below, test results from a total of 6,733 panelists were used in the September 2012 Report.

[57] The speed tiers measured in the 2012 study are described in detail in the Technical Appendix at 28-29.

[58] Measurement Lab (M-Lab) is an open, distributed server platform for researchers to deploy Internet measurement tools.

[59] Ultra High Definition television is a term coined by industry groups to define a next generation television standard and set of supporting products. Minimum performance attributes include display resolution of at least eight million active pixels, with at least 3,840 horizontally and at least 2,160 vertically. Displays will have an aspect ratio with width to height of at least 16x9. See Consumer Electronic Association announcement at http://www.ce.org/News/News-Releases/Press-Releases/2012-Press-Releases/Consumer-Electronics-Industry-Announces-Ultra-High.aspx (last accessed January 12, 2013).

[60] Available at fcc.us/mba0213rawbulkdataset.

www.ingramcontent.com/pod-product-compliance
Lightning Source LLC
Chambersburg PA
CBHW050801180526
45159CB00004B/1516